Health Care
Law and Ethics

Workbook to accompany

Health Care Law and Ethics

American Association of Medical Assistants
Chicago

Workbook to accompany
Health Care Law and Ethics

Published by the
American Association of Medical Assistants, Inc.
20 North Wacker Drive, Suite 1575
Chicago, Illinois 60606-2903

This is a revised edition of the workbook to accompany *Law for the Medical Office*, a workbook previously published by the American Association of Medical Assistants, Inc.

ISBN Number: 0-942732-03-0

Table of Contents

How to Use This Workbook

This workbook is provided with the firm conviction that it is easier to learn these concepts if the material is presented in a variety of ways. There are many opportunities for you to test what you are learning as you progress through the course.

Each workbook chapter includes several types of personal practice exercises.

The programmed review is keyed very closely to the material developed in the text. It is your primary tool for review and study. It consists of a number of fill-in items, the answers to which appear in the margin. Two options are available to you as you work through this section: (1) cover the answers and record them in the space provided; or (2) cover the answers, and record your responses in a notebook. The latter option will allow you to study the material over and over.

Many chapters contain matching exercises. You should match the terms in the left-hand column with the letter corresponding to the correct definition or description in the right-hand column.

You should respond to the completion/essay exercises in writing. You may use the space provided, or record your responses in a notebook. Writing is important here; it will reinforce the concepts and procedures.

The quiz should be used when you have completed studying each chapter, responded to all the competency checks, and are able to correctly complete the programmed review, matching, and essay exercises. On the multiple choice items, you should circle the letter corresponding to the one best ending or response.

The answer key following the personal practice exercises at the end of each chapter provides the correct responses to all chapter exercises and the quizzes.

At the end of the workbook—following Chapter 14—there is a final examination. You should take this examination without referring to your book. If you purchased the book through an educational institution, you are not eligible for Continuing Education Unit credit. If you purchased your course through AAMA, you may be eligible for CEU credit providing:

- You complete the test answer sheet as the instructions indicate.
- You achieve an average score of 70 percent or better on the test.
- You return the answer sheet to AAMA with your name, address, and Social Security number printed legibly.

If you have any questions on the materials provided, or the procedures for obtaining your CEU credit, please contact AAMA staff in the Continuing Education Department.

1
An Introduction To Law

PERSONAL PRACTICE EXERCISES

PROGRAMMED REVIEW

Instructions:
Cover the words in the left-hand margin with a piece of paper. Read the material that follows, filling in the blanks before uncovering the answers. Study this section carefully before proceeding to the next exercise. If you have any questions, reread the corresponding portion of the chapter in your text.

law

physical / social

Whether referred to as rules, traditions, or regulations, the purpose of _____ is to govern certain aspects of social behavior in a binding way. This ensures the _____ and _____ survival of the group.

public
civil

In the United States, laws can be divided into two major categories. The rights and responsibilities of the government to its citizens and the citizens to its government are defined in _____ law. Private law, which governs certain activities between and among private citizens, is sometimes referred to as _____ law.

statutes
statutory / public
law

There are two sources of laws. Legislators at both the state and federal levels enact laws known as _____. These are periodically compiled and published as codes. This is known as _____ law. To a large degree, _____ _____ is now based upon statutory law.

common law

stare decisis

Judge-made laws, better known as _____ _____, are legal precedents established by judicial decisions. Such precedents are followed by other judges until they are overruled by a court of higher authority. This principle is called _____ _____, which means "the previous decision stands."

public

Criminal, constitutional, administrative and international law are all branches of _____ law.

contract
tort / corporation

Private law is comprised of six branches: property, inheritance, family, _____, _____ and _____ law.

tort

A "tort" is a private or civil wrong resulting from the breach of legal duty, but excluding breaches of contract. The redress of injuries suffered by one person because of another's misdeed is the purpose of _____ law.

contract law	The rights and obligations of people who enter into contractual relationships are the subject of _____ _____.
contract law	The physician-patient relationship is governed by _____ _____.
tort	However, most lawsuits against physicians and other health care practitioners which are based on "negligence" fall within _____ law.
substantive	Law may also be categorized as substantive or procedural. The rights and responsibilities of parties in legal relationships are described in _____ law. Public health law requirements on reporting communicable diseases are examples of
substantive laws	_____ _____.
procedural	Procedural law sets forth the rules by which disputes may be settled in a fair and just manner. Based on the adversary process, _____ law positions opposing sides against each other. Each side is granted the opportunity to prove its story and/or disprove the story of the other party. The litigation process is part of
procedural	_____ law.
substantive procedural	A physician is required to have and use reasonable skill in treating patients. This section of private law deals with the legal relationships between physician and patient. It is an example of _____ law. If a patient sues the physician, the laws governing actions taken in the litigation process would be _____.

MATCHING

Instructions:
Match the terms in the left-hand column with the letter corresponding to the correct definitions or descriptions in the right-hand column. The answer key appears at the end of this chapter.

1. ____ common law
   ____ contract law
   ____ private law
   ____ procedural law
   ____ statutory law
   ____ tort law

a. also called civil law, it governs certain activities between or among individuals
b. based on the adversary process, it sets forth the rules by which disputes may be settled fairly
c. concerns the formation and operation of incorporated businesses (physicians who are incorporated must be concerned with these laws)
d. establishes the respective rights of survivors and sets rules for making wills
e. governs in part the physician-patient relationship
f. governs the redress of injuries suffered because of someone else's negligence—the basis of most lawsuits against physicians
g. governs the responsibilities of government to its citizens
h. legal precedent established by judicial decision, which may be changed by judicial decision or statute
i. rules enacted by legislatures—to a large degree the basis of public law

COMPLETION/ESSAY

Instructions:
Respond to the following directions in writing. Doing so will reinforce the concepts and procedures present-ed in Chapter 1 of the text. The answer key appears at the end of this chapter of the workbook.

1. List the four branches of public law.
   a.
   b.
   c.
   d.

2. Give an example that characterizes actions governed by each of the four branches you listed in "1."
   a.
   b.
   c.
   d.

3. List the six branches of private law.
   a.
   b.
   c.
   d.
   e.
   f.

4. Give an example that characterizes actions governed by each of the six branches you listed in "3."
   a.
   b.
   c.
   d.
   e.
   f.

QUIZ

Instructions:
Select and then circle the letter corresponding to the one best ending or response to each of the following statements or questions. The answer key appears at the end of this chapter.

1. The body that reviews a trial court's decision when the losing side disputes a question of law is the
   a. appellate court
   b. Board of Medical Examiners
   c. district court
   d. municipal court
   e. trial court

2. The rights and responsibilities of government to its citizens and citizens to the government are defined in
   a. administrative law
   b. inheritance law
   c. property law
   d. public law
   e. tort law

3. Common law decisions are
   a. based on statutes known as codes
   b. decisions rendered in lower courts
   c. legal precedents established by judicial decision
   d. rules established by administrative agencies
   e. trial court decisions upheld by appellate courts

4. An intermediate appellate court
   a. automatically reviews all suits settled in lower court
   b. has final jurisdiction over any lawsuit
   c. has original jurisdiction over suits between residents of different states
   d. must reach a unanimous decision in order to reverse a trial court decision
   e. reviews trial court decisions when the losing side disputes a point of law decided by the trial judge

5. The increased number of lawsuits against physicians has been attributed to the
   a. courts' ability to handle increased caseload
   b. breakdown in rapport between physicians and patients
   c. higher costs of medical care
   d. decreased use of high risk procedures

6. Statutory law
   a. is commonly referred to as judge-made law
   b. has its greatest impact in private law
   c. is based upon precedent
   d. is periodically compiled and published as codes

7. Private law includes
   a. administrative law
   b. constitutional law
   c. criminal law
   d. tort law

ANSWERS TO EXERCISES

MATCHING

1. h
   e
   a
   b
   i
   f

COMPLETION/ESSAY

1. a. criminal
   b. constitutional
   c. administrative
   d. international

2. a. Criminal law defines crimes, describes penalties for offenses, and stipulates procedures for prosecuting offenders.
   b. Constitutional law defines the rights, responsibilities, and powers of government and citizens.
   c. Administrative law describes the rights and powers of government agencies.
   d. International law deals with treaties and agreements between and among countries, such as trade agreements.

3. a. contract
   b. tort
   c. property
   d. family
   e. corporation
   f. inheritance

4. a. Contract law concerns the rights and obligations of people who enter into contracts.
   b. Tort law governs the redress of wrongs or injuries suffered by someone because of another's wrongdoing or misdeed.
   c. Property law governs the ownership of real and personal property.
   d. Family law specifies the rights and obligations of husbands and wives, children and parents.
   e. Corporation law concerns the formation and operation of incorporated businesses.
   f. Inheritance law concerns the transfer of property after the owner's death.

QUIZ

1. a
2. d
3. c
4. e
5. b
6. d
7. d

2

Licensure and Certification

PROGRAMMED REVIEW

Instructions:
Cover the words in the left-hand margin with a piece of paper. Read the material that follows, filling in the blanks before uncovering the answers. Study this section carefully before proceeding to the next exercise. If you have any questions, reread the corresponding portion of the chapter in your text.

reciprocity
endorsement

Physicians may be granted licenses in three ways: through (1) meeting the requirements of the Medical Practice Act; (2) _____, when a state recognizes a license granted by another state; or (3) _____, when a state has reviewed the physician's credentials and/or test results.

revoked

Medical Practice Acts set forth grounds and procedures for revoking and suspending physicians' licenses. The term revoking means taking away, or calling back. When the state withdraws the physician's right to practice medicine, it has _____ his/her license.

suspended

When a license is suspended, the physician is stopped, temporarily, from practicing medicine in that state. The physician does not lose the license itself. He/she loses only the right to practice medicine for a specific period of time. If a physician is stopped from practicing medicine, but only for a time, his/her license has been _____.

revoked / suspended

A criminal offense, unprofessional conduct, fraud, or professional incompetence may be grounds for a license to be either _____ or _____. A criminal offense is usually cause for revocation of a license. Tax evasion, murder, rape, violating narcotics laws are all examples of criminal offenses.

gross immorality

unprofessional

Unprofessional conduct covers a variety of offenses. Some states use the term gross immorality in lieu of unprofessional conduct. When an action does not meet the standards of behavior accepted by other physicians in the community, it is called unprofessional conduct or _____ _____. Betrayal of a physician-patient confidence and assisting an unlicensed person to practice medicine are examples of _____ conduct.

suspension
fraudulent
fraud
fraud

Fraud is cause for revocation of a license in some states, but in others it is only considered cause for _____. For an act to be considered fraudulent, it must involve intent to deceive. Submitting a bill to a government agency claiming that services were rendered when they were not is a _____. Intentionally misrepresenting the ability to cure a patient's ailment is _____.

ordinary

Physicians declared mentally incompetent may have their licenses revoked on the grounds of professional incompetence. Usually, decisions of incompetence are based upon repeated charges of gross negligence. A distinction is made between ordinary negligence and gross negligence. A single case of mistaken judgment is ordinary negligence. A license would not be revoked for a single case of mistaken judgment, or _____ negligence. But conduct that has shown a high disregard for human welfare is gross negligence. High disregard, or repeated disregard for human welfare can result in a revoked license.

license

Besides physicians, many other health care providers must also possess a state _____ before they may practice their profession. The license indicates that the professional has met minimum standards prescribed by the state.

certification / certified

Some physicians have also become certified within their chosen specialty. Certification is awarded to recognize specific skills in specific areas of practice. Licensure is mandatory; _____ is voluntary. No state requires a physician to be _____.

certification

Certification verifies that a person has met specific requirements. A Certified Medical Assistant (CMA) credential is evidence that the person has successfully completed a national examination testing knowledge in all aspects of the profession. In fields like medical assisting, _____ is evidence that a particular level of qualification has been attained.

license

certification

When an individual is both licensed and certified, the _____ often indicates a minimum standard of competence, and the higher level of competence is indicated by the _____. In some occupations for which no license is required, certification can also refer to a minimum level of competence.

license

certification

When a state grants a physician or another health care provider the right to practice, the professional has been granted a _____. When a specialty board tests a professional's competence in a specific field and verifies that the person is qualified to perform specific tasks and functions, the person has received _____.

MATCHING

Instructions:
Match the terms in the left-hand column with the letter corresponding to the correct definitions or descriptions in the right-hand column. The answer key appears at the end of this chapter.

1. ___ revocation
2. ___ reciprocity
3. ___ fraud
4. ___ certification

    a. indicates that the professional has met the minimum standards prescribed by the state
    b. taking away of a right or privilege
    c. stipulates how practitioners can perform their duties
    d. punishable for one or more years in prison, usually a cause for revocation of license
    e. recognition of specific skills in specific areas of practice
    f. sometimes termed "gross immorality," it is action that does not meet standards of behavior of other physicians
    g. allows a physician already licensed in one state to practice in another
    h. intent to deceive

SHORT ESSAY

Instructions:
Write a short essay in response to the directions given in the following statements. Use the space provided for your answers. The answer key appears at the end of this chapter.

1. Identify the three ways in which physicians may be granted licenses:
   a.
   b.
   c.

2. Specify four grounds on which a license may be either revoked or suspended:
   a.
   b.
   c.
   d.

3. Give four examples of unprofessional conduct:
   a.
   b.
   c.
   d.

4. Explain the differences between gross negligence and ordinary negligence.

5. Explain the differences between licensure and certification.

6. Name three aspects of licensure of concern today:
   a.
   b.
   c.

QUIZ

Instructions:
Select and then circle the letter corresponding to the one best ending or response to each of the following statements or questions. The answer key appears at the end of this chapter.

1. An act performed by a physician is considered fraudulent when
   a. it was an honest mistake
   b. it was an inadvertent misrepresentation
   c. it involved an intent to deceive
   d. All of the above

2. License revocation is automatic in the case of
   a. tax evasion
   b. murder
   c. any conviction related to medical malpractice
   d. under no circumstance

3. Under the Medical Practice Act, the body/bodies authorized to grant license(s) to practice medicine is/are the:
   a. State Boards of Medical Examiners.
   b. American Medical Association
   c. National Board of Medical Examiners
   d. None of the above

4. One example of a fraudulent act is
   a. filing false Medicare forms
   b. misrepresenting the ability to cure a patient's ailment
   c. submitting a bill to a governmental agency claiming that services were rendered, when they were not
   d. All of the above

5. Specialty certification of a physician
   a. results in automatic licensure by the physician's home state
   b. demonstrates a higher standard of competency than a state license
   c. is administered by the state medical licensing board

ANSWERS TO EXERCISES

MATCHING

1. b
2. g
3. h
4. e

SHORT ESSAY

1. a. meeting the requirements of the Medical Practice Act
   b. reciprocity
   c. endorsement

2. a. criminal offenses
   b. unprofessional conduct
   c. fraud
   d. professional incompetence

3. a. willful betrayal of a physician-patient confidence
   b. substance abuse
   c. sexual misbehavior
   d. assistance of an unlicensed and untrained person in the practice of medicine

4. Gross negligence is a high disregard for human welfare, conduct of a reckless nature, or failure to use slight care when dealing with other people. Ordinary negligence is failure to use care that a reasonable person would use; in other words, an honest mistake.

5. Licensure means that a professional has met minimum standards set by the state. Licensure is mandatory. Certification is a voluntary process awarded to recognize specific skills in specific areas of practice.

6. a. poorly-defined categories
   b. fragmentation of responsibilities among examining boards, state departments of health and regulatory authorities
   c. obstacles to career

QUIZ

1. c
2. d
3. a
4. d
5. b

3

The Doctor–Patient Relationship

PERSONAL PRACTICE EXERCISES

PROGRAMMED REVIEW

Instructions:
Cover the words in the left-hand margin with a piece of paper. Read the material that follows, filling in the blanks before uncovering the answers. Study this section carefully before proceeding to the next exercise. If you have any questions, reread the corresponding portion of the chapter in your text.

right
treatment

right / treatment
patient

In the doctor–patient relationship, the patient and the doctor have rights. The patient has the _____ to choose the doctor he/she wishes to treat him/her. The patient also has the right to limit treatment. He/she can refuse _____, or he/she can set limits on the care provided. In the patient's general right to limit treatment he/she has the _____ to give an informed consent to _____. The_____ has the right to know what the treatment will consist of, the dangers of the treatment, and what effect it will have on his/her body.

physician

right

Physicians in private practice have rights, also. Physicians have the right to choose patients. Provided certain guidelines are followed, the _____ can refuse service to new patients or to former patients with new problems. Physicians also have the _____ to stipulate services and conditions under which their services will be provided.

legal

offer
acceptance

consideration

compensate

The physician-patient contract contains certain elements found in all legal contracts. Five elements of a _____ contract are offer, acceptance, consideration, capacity, and legality of subject matter. The patient's entry into the physician's office implies he/she is seeking the services of the physician. This is the first part of the legal contract, referred to as the _____. When the physician agrees to provide service, he/she has accepted the patient. The physician's _____ can be implied from his/her willingness to provide the service. The third element of the legal contract is the _____, the mutual exchange of promises. The physician and the patient agree to fulfill contractual obligations. The patient promises to _____ the physician for services rendered.

contract
competent
another person

The fourth essential element is the legal capacity to _____. This means that the parties to the contract are mentally _____ adults. Minors and incompetent adults require _____ _____ to act on their behalf. The final element is

legal
breaking

_____ subject matter. The subject of the contract must be lawful; it would not be valid if it involved _____ a law.

obligation
standard
physician
obligation

Upon establishment of the physician-patient relationship, each party incurs certain obligations. The physician's _____ is the "standard of care." The patient is owed the _____ of care. This means that skill, knowledge, and experience of the _____ must be at least average, when compared to like physicians in the same circumstances. A specific _____ assumed by the physician once the re-lationship with the patient is established is to treat the patient until the condition no longer requires medical treatment or until a proper withdrawal or discharge is made.

obligated

The physician must obtain informed consent before proceeding. He/she is _____ to caution patients against unneeded or undesirable surgery. He/she must give

complete

_____ instructions and respect the patient's privacy and the confidential nature of the physician-patient relationship.

reasonable
guarantee
guarantees
contract

The physician's contractual obligations only guarantee the patient that the physician will have and will exercise _____ skill, knowledge, and experience. There is no _____ as to the results unless such guarantees are expressly made. A physician is not prohibited from making any _____. However, specific promises not kept will subject the physician to a breach of _____ suit.

obligations

In the physician-patient contract, the patient has contractual _____ as does the physician. The patient is obligated to accurately and truthfully report his/her history

physician/contractual
pay

and symptoms to the _____. Other _____ obligations of the patient are to follow the physician's instructions and to _____ for the services ren-dered.

implied / terminates

reason

withdrawal
physician

The contractual physician-patient relationship can be terminated expressly or by implication. When the need for treatment ceases, the termination of the contract is _____. If the physician _____ the contract, his/her intent should be expressed in a letter. The letter of withdrawal from the case should state the _____ for termination. The physician should advise the patient to seek further medical care within a reasonable time, if the patient's condition so requires. The physician should also offer cooperation in providing information from the patient's medical record. This letter of _____ should be signed by the _____ and should be sent certified mail with return receipt requested.

terminated

physician
record
certified

The physician-patient contractual relationship may be _____ by the patient. If this termination is verbal, the physician should send a letter to the patient con-firming the discharge. Again, he/she should advise the patient to obtain another _____ if the medical condition requires. He/she should extend cooperation in providing information from the patient's medical _____. The letter should be signed by the physician and sent _____ mail, return receipt requested.

notice

substitute

The physician who withdraws from a case without terminating the relationship may be sued for abandonment. Another basis for a suit may be physician withdrawal from the case without _____ to the patient. A charge of abandonment may be made if the physician errs regarding the patient's need for continued treat-ment or fails to see the patient often enough. If the physician fails to provide a qual-ified _____ during periods of unavailability, he/she may be charged with abandonment. In the physician-patient relationship there are some special situations to be considered. They are the treatment of minors, assessment examinations, and

minors

emergencies. In the treatment of _____, the minor-patient is owed the stan-

obligations

dard of care. The parent or legal guardian is responsible for the minor's _____ to the physician, including payment of the physician's fee. Parents of an emancipated minor are not responsible for the cost of the minor's care. An emancipated minor is a minor child who has voluntarily left his/her parents' home for the purpose of supporting himself/herself and living independently. An emancipated minor is

fee

responsible for the physician's _____.

contract

When a person is being examined at the request of an insurance company, the _____ between the physician and the examinee is usually not established.

contract

An assessment examination of a litigant by the court-appointed physician is another example of a special situation in which the _____ between the physician and examinee is not established.

implied

A limited implied contract may exist in an emergency situation. The emergency victim's request for treatment and consent may be _____, as must his/her promise

compensate

to _____ the physician for services rendered. In the limited implied contract,

limited

the physician's obligations are _____ to rendering treatment until the patient

limited

can be turned over to a competent medical authority. During the time the _____ implied contract is in effect, the physician is obligated to provide the standard of

standard

care. The _____ of care is the care that is provided by similar physicians

similar

under _____ emergency conditions.

laws

Good Samaritan laws have been enacted in most states. Good Samaritan _____ have been enacted to encourage health care providers to render aid at the scene of

Samaritans

an accident or emergency. These laws exempt "Good _____" from liability for ordinary professional negligence.

COMPLETION

Instructions:
Fill in the words or phrases that will correctly complete the following statements. The answer key appears at the end of this chapter.

1. Two rights of patients are
   a.
   b.

2. Two rights of physicians are
   a.
   b.

3. In the "standard of care," the physician's _____, _____ and _____ must be at least average when compared to like physicians in the same circumstances.

4. The five specific physician's contractual obligations are
   a.
   b.
   c.
   d.
   e.

5. _____ is defined as the physician's unilateral withdrawal, without adequate notice, from caring for a patient whose condition requires medical treatment.

QUIZ

Instructions:
Select and then circle the letter corresponding to the one best ending or response to each of the following statements or questions. The answer key appears at the end of this chapter.

1. The responsibility for the medical bills of an emancipated minor belongs to the
   a. emancipated minor
   b. closest relative
   c. grandparent
   d. guardian
   e. parent

2. An emancipated minor is a person under 18 who is
   a. a ward of the court
   b. dependent on the state for support
   c. enrolled in a school providing postsecondary education
   d. legally responsible for his/her own debts
   e. living away from home, but still dependent on his/her parents for financial support

3. In recommending a face-lift operation, a cosmetic surgeon told a patient that the operation would make her look 15 years younger. His/her comment could be construed as
   a. a warranty as to result
   b. an implied contract
   c. negligence
   d. *res ipsa loquitur*
   e. the standard of care

4. The patient in the foregoing incident proceeded with the face-lift operation. Although the surgeon exercised exceptionally good skill in executing the procedure, the patient's face was permanently disfigured because of some personal idiosyncratic reaction to the procedure. Of the following grounds for a lawsuit, the surgeon would most likely be liable for
   a. assault and battery
   b. breach of contract
   c. invasion of the patient's privacy
   d. ordinary negligence
   e. nothing because the disfigurement was not his/her fault

5. An essential element of a legal contract is the
   a. the contract being written
   b. rejection
   c. acceptance
   d. nonconsideration

6. The "standard of care" means the physician must have and use reasonable
   a. empathy
   b. sympathy
   c. patience
   d. knowledge

7. Once the physician-patient relationship is established, the physician is obliged to treat the patient

   a. only if the patient prepays
   b. after the patient discharges the physician
   c. until the physician expressly withdraws

ANSWERS TO EXERCISES

COMPLETION

1. a. to choose the physician
   b. to limit treatment

2. a. to choose patients
   b. to stipulate services and the conditions under which services will be provided

3. skill, experience, knowledge

4. a. treat the patient until the condition no longer requires medical treatment or until the contract is expressly terminated
   b. obtain informed consent before proceeding
   c. caution patients against unneeded or undesirable surgery
   d. give the patient complete instructions
   e. respect the patient's privacy and the confidential nature of the physician-patient relationship

5. Abandonment

QUIZ

1. a
2. d
3. a
4. b
5. c
6. d
7. c

4

Confidentiality in the Doctor–Patient Relationship

PERSONAL PRACTICE EXERCISES

PROGRAMMED REVIEW

Instructions:
Cover the words in the left-hand margin with a piece of paper. Read the material that follows, filling in the blanks before uncovering the answers. Study this section carefully before proceeding to the next exercise. If you have any questions, reread the corresponding portion of the chapter in your text.

law / Confidentiality

principle
unethical
unlawful

The physician-patient relationship is confidential, ethically and legally. Information obtained in the care of the patient must not be revealed without the permission of the patient unless required by _____. _____ of patient information is an ethical principle of the medical profession. All health care professionals must abide by the same _____. Revealing confidential information is referred to as unauthorized disclosure. Disclosing confidential information is both _____ and _____.

statutes

Privileged commu-
nication
confidentiality
suing / testifying

Many states have enacted privileged communication statutes. These _____ prohibit physicians from testifying in court without the patient's consent or without a waiver of right to confidentiality. _____ _____ statutes are meant to protect the patient and his/her interests. Such statutes are enacted to protect the _____ of physician-patient communications. The patient may waive the right to confidentiality by _____ the physician or by _____ voluntarily.

law
disclosure

authorization

authorization
filed

Disclosure of information is the patient's choice unless required by _____. Authorization for _____ of information should be written and filed in the patient's medical record. The authorization should contain the name of the physician being authorized, the name of the intended recipient, and the date on which the treatment began. A statement authorizing the physician to testify and waiving the patient's right to confidentiality should also be a part of the _____ for disclosure. The patient's signature, date and place of signing, and the signature of a witness are items of verification of the authenticity of the authorization. Each time the patient requests disclosure of information, a separate _____ must be obtained and _____ in the patient's medical record.

kept
outside
other patients

Health care professionals must take certain precautions to prevent accidental disclosure of information. Medical office records must be _____ from curious eyes. Patients must never be discussed _____ the office or in the presence of _____ _____ inside the office. Health care professionals should discuss patients only with individuals who are entitled to the information.

legally required

Legally required disclosures are those disclosures that come about as the result of the public's right to certain information. These _____ _____ disclosures are categorized as disclosures that are required by subpoena, required by statute to protect health, or necessary to protect the welfare of the patient or of a third party. A subpoena is a court order requiring the recipient to appear at a certain time and

subpoena duces tecum place in order to testify. A _____ _____ _____ requires that the record be brought to court with the recipient.

law / births

The physician is required by _____ to report _____ and deaths. Public health statutes require that acts of violence, incidences of certain contagious, infectious, and communicable diseases, and incidences of known drug addiction must be reported to a specified person or agency.

disclosure / third
disclosed

disclosed

Protection of the welfare of the patient or of a third party is another category of legally required _____. When the _____ party's well-being is endangered, the physician may have the duty to disclose the information. This _____ information should be limited to persons with a legitimate right to, or need for, the information that the physician can release in good faith and with reasonable confidence in its accuracy. Information _____ should be limited to that which is necessary to accomplish the objective and that which can be fairly reported.

statute
privacy

consent

The patient's right to privacy has been recognized by _____ or common law in most states. The right to _____ means that the patient's written consent be obtained before photographs are taken or before the patient's condition receives any publicity. Observers are not permitted during the examination or treatment until the patient's _____ is obtained.

MATCHING

Instructions:
Match the terms in the left-hand column with the letter corresponding to the correct definitions or descriptions in the right-hand column. The answer key appears at the end of this chapter.

1. ____ statute
    ____ subpoena
    ____ right to privacy
    ____ *subpoena duces tecum*
    ____ unauthorized disclosure
    ____ confidential information

a. court order to appear
b. court order to appear with record
c. information obtained during treatment
d. law enacted by a legislative body
e. betrayal of a professional confidence
f. principle entitling individual to be free of unwanted publicity

COMPLETION

Instructions:
Fill in the words or phrases that will correctly complete the following statements. The answer key appears at the end of this chapter.

1. The purpose of privileged communication statutes is

2. A patient may waive the right to privacy by
   a.
   b.

3. How should inquiries from well-meaning friends and relatives of a patient be handled?

4. List four precautionary measures that may be used to prevent accidental disclosure
   a.
   b.
   c.
   d.

5. Three categories of legally required disclosures are those
   a.
   b.
   c.

6. The literal translation of *subpoena duces tecum* is

7. Four events or situations that a physician is required by statute to disclose to protect public health or welfare are
   a.
   b.
   c.
   d.

8. With respect to medical treatment, the patient's right to privacy generally requires that written consent be given before
   a.
   b.
   c.

QUIZ

Instructions:
Select and then circle the letter corresponding to the one best ending or response to each of the following statements or questions. The answer key appears at the end of this chapter.

1. Privileged communication statutes are meant to protect the
   a. physician
   b. physician's employees
   c. patient
   d. third parties

2. A subpoena is
   a. a court order notifying the recipient he/she is a defendant in a lawsuit
   b. a court order requiring the recipient to appear at a certain time and place to testify
   c. a written statement setting forth the plaintiff's allegation against a defendant
   d. a list of questions served on a defendant that requires a written response
   e. the defendant's written response to a plaintiff's complaint

3. A legally effective form authorizing a physician to release patient medical information contains the
   a. patient's agreement to pay for processing costs
   b. name of the patient's lawyer
   c. name of the doctor authorized to release the information
   d. patient's complete medical history

ANSWERS TO EXERCISES

MATCHING

1. d
   a
   f
   b
   e
   c

COMPLETION/ESSAY

1. to protect the confidentiality of physician-patient communications

2. a. suing the physician
   b. testifying voluntarily

3. Inquiries should be handled politely but firmly and should be refused.

4. a. Never discuss patients outside the office or in front of other patients in the office
   b. Converse with patients in private
   c. Keep the appointment book, patient files, and patient records out of public view
   d. Discuss patients only with those in need of and entitled to the information

5. a. required by subpoena
   b. required by statute to protect the public health or welfare
   c. necessary to protect the welfare of the patient or a third party

6. "under penalty you shall take it with you"

7. a. births and deaths
   b. acts of violence
   c. contagious, infectious, or communicable diseases
   d. known drug addicts

8. a. public disclosure
   b. observers are permitted during examination and treatment
   c. photographs are taken

QUIZ

1. c
2. b
3. c

5

Consent to Medical Treatment

PERSONAL PRACTICE EXERCISES

PROGRAMMED REVIEW

Instructions:
Cover the words in the left-hand margin with a piece of paper. Read the material that follows, filling in the blanks before uncovering the answers. Study this section carefully before proceeding to the next exercise. If you have any questions, reread the corresponding portion of the chapter in your text.

fiduciary **relationship** **professional** **fiduciary** **professional** **risks**	A fiduciary relationship is a relationship between certain highly trained, service-oriented professionals and persons seeking their services. The relationship between attorney/client and physician/patient—for example—is a _____ relationship. The fiduciary _____ is based on the client's trust and confidence in the professional's knowledge and ability. This relationship obligates the _____ to act in the best interest of the client. The _____ relationship obligates the _____ to disclose voluntarily all information relevant to the service being offered, including inherent defects and _____.
Informed **proposed** **patient** **informed** **patient** **alternative / probable**	Informed consent is required before the treatment begins. _____ consent stems from the patient's genuine understanding of the nature of the _____ treatment and predictable results. The _____ must understand the known risks and hazards inherent in the treatment and the likelihood of their occurrence before he/she can give _____ consent. Side effects or consequences known to occur with some regularity, their severity, and their permanence must be understood by the _____. In order to give informed consent, the patient must understand _____ treatments and _____ outcomes of each.
greater **physicians** **experimental** **known** **understandable** **patient**	There are some guidelines for physicians to follow concerning disclosures. The greater the risk involved, in terms of likelihood of occurrence, permanence, or severity, the _____ the physician's obligation to disclose it. Alternative treatment recommended by at least a respectable number of reasonable _____ should be disclosed. If the proposed treatment is unconventional or experimental, the patient should be explicitly informed that it is unconventional or _____ and that all risks may not be _____. Reasonable measures should be taken to ensure the patient's understanding of the physician's explanation. Terms _____ and meaningful to each patient should be used. An atmosphere of open and candid communication between the physician and _____ should be fostered.

communication
spouse

risks
high risk
therapy
patient / withheld

risks

Two-way _____ should be encouraged. Provided the patient consents, the patient's _____ should be included in the discussion of recommended treatment. A physician may justifiably withhold information from a patient for therapeutic reasons. Known _____ and alternative treatments should be given to the patient's spouse or next of kin. Certain _____ procedures, such as chemotherapy, electroshock therapy, and radiation _____ should always be explained to the _____. Information can be _____ when the patient persistently and obviously refuses to listen or states that he/she does not want to know about the procedure or the _____ involved.

informed
emergency
consent

patient

The doctrine of _____ consent poses special concerns for the physician. In _____ situations, operations may be extended to remove the threat to life or limb on the grounds that the patient's _____ is implied. In nonemergency situations, operations may be extended if the extension is considered good surgical practice or if it is in the best interest of the _____.

precautionary
consent
spouse

patient
precautionary

Precautionary measures should be taken to reduce the surgeon's liability for extending the operation beyond the patient's express consent. One _____ measure is to have the presurgical written _____ of the patient authorize the surgeon to correct any unanticipated problems. If the patient's _____ or next of kin is available, the surgeon should explain the need for extending the operation, and obtain the consent on behalf of the _____. Another _____ measure to reduce the surgeon's liability is to have a presurgical agreement with the patient on how the surgeon will proceed if the extension involves the patient's sexual or reproductive organs.

risks
negligence
revised
legitimate

risk / material

profession

A physician who treats a patient without permission may be sued for assault and battery. The physician who obtains a patient's consent, but does not properly explain the inherent _____ of treatment may be sued for professional negligence. In order to have a legitimate case based on _____, the patient must show that he/she would not have _____ the treatment had he/she been properly informed. To have a _____ case, the patient must show that it was the practice of other physicians in the community to disclose the risk or that the _____ was a material one that should have been explained. A _____ risk is one a "reasonable person" would consider significant. This doctrine is known as the Canterbury Rule. The doctrine also says that the right of a patient to information should not be determined by the customs of a _____.

consent
authority
authority

parent
sexually transmitted
treatment
debts
authority
minor

In considering the consent to medical treatment, we must look at who has the authority to _____. Mentally competent adults who are not delirious, comatose, or under the influence of drugs or alcohol have the _____ to consent to treatment. For most conditions, the parent or legal guardian of a minor has this _____. When parents are separated or divorced, the consent to medical treatment must be obtained from the custodial _____. In many states, minors may be treated for _____ _____ disease or drug addiction without parental consent. An emancipated minor may consent to medical _____ and is responsible for his/her own _____. The spouse, parent, or court-appointed guardian of an incompetent adult has _____ to consent to treatment. When a parent or guardian refuses treatment of a _____ for life- or limb- threatening conditions out of neglect, ignorance, or religious belief, the authority to consent may be a court order.

Implied	The two forms of consent to medical treatment are implied and express. _____ consent is the form of consent implied by the patient's behavior and actions. Implied consent is considered sufficient legal protection for the physician in the treatment of
standardized	minor routine problems, when the treatment is _____ throughout the profes-
negligible	sion and is of _____ risk.
Express / express	_____ consent is specific oral or written permission. Written _____ consent
surgery	is recommended whenever treatment involves _____, high risk procedures,
Written	or experimental drugs or procedures. _____ express consent can reduce the
physician	possibility of misunderstanding between the _____ and the patient.
express	The effective written _____ consent form contains several important items. It should contain a brief description of the proposed procedure, along with the name
physician	of the _____ being authorized to perform the procedure. The authorization to extend the procedure, if necessary in the physician's judgment, should be stated in
consent form	the _____ _____. The written consent form should contain the oppor- tunity to prohibit certain types of anesthesia and the opportunity for the patient to
informed	limit publicity. The statement should indicate that the patient's consent is _____
guaranteed consent	and that the results are not _____. The _____ form should be dated,
signature	should bear the _____ of the person legally qualified to give consent, and
witness	should be signed by a _____.

MATCHING

Instructions:
Match the terms in the left-hand column with the letter corresponding to the correct definitions or descriptions in the right-hand column. The answer key appears at the end of this chapter.

1. ___ assault and battery
   ___ blanket consent
   ___ Canterbury Rule
   ___ express consent
   ___ fiduciary
   ___ implied consent
   ___ material risk

   a. let the buyer beware
   b. specific oral or written permission
   c. a reasonable person would consider significant
   d. patient alleges no authorization for treatment
   e. consent for non-specific procedures
   f. inherent risks not properly disclosed
   g. the right of a patient to information should not be determined by the customs of a profession
   h. entity holding a thing in trust
   i. consent by behavior and actions

COMPLETION

Instructions:
Fill in the words or phrases that will correctly complete the following statements. The answer key appears at the end of this chapter.

1. The _____ the risk involved, in terms of likelihood of occurrence, permanence, or severity, the _____ the physician's obligation to disclose it.

2. A/An _____ relationship is based on the client's trust and confidence in the professional's knowledge.

3. "_____ _____" means let the buyer beware.

4. A/An _____ risk is one a "reasonable person" would consider significant.

5. The _____ Rule says that, since the patient has the sole right to decide whether to have treatment, his/her right to information should not be determined by the medical profession.

6. A physician who treats a patient without permission may be sued for _____ and _____.

7. A physician who obtains a patient's consent, but does not properly explain risks inherent in the proposed treatment, may be sued on the grounds of professional _____.

8. Consent demonstrated by behavior and actions is _____ consent.

9. A/An _____ minor may consent to medical treatment and is responsible for his/her own debts.

10. When parents are separated or divorced, the consent of the _____ parent is required before the minor receives treatment, except in an emergency.

QUIZ

Instructions:
Select and then circle the letter corresponding to the one best ending or response to each of the following statements or questions. The answer key appears at the end of this chapter.

1. In a fiduciary relationship, the professional is obligated to
   a. act in the best interest of the client
   b. act in the best interest of his/her peers
   c. disclose voluntarily all information relevant to the treatment except risks
   d. follow the doctrine of "caveat emptor"

2. A court that adheres to the theory of the Canterbury Rule will require physicians to
   a. withhold information from patients for therapeutic reasons
   b. obtain a court order before withdrawing lifesaving treatment on elderly patients with terminal illness
   c. disclose inherent risks with a statistical probability of five percent or greater of occurring
   d. disclose inherent risks that a reasonable person would consider significant
   e. disclose inherent risks according to the practices of reputable physicians in the same community

3. In most suits against physicians for assault and battery, the plaintiffs allege that the defendants
    a. did not properly inform them of risks inherent in proposed treatments
    b. did not meet the standard of care required by their contract
    c. failed to see them as often as their conditions required
    d. treated them without authorization
    e. did not inform them of material risks.

4. A patient's express written consent should be obtained before a physician
    a. authorizes a prescription refill
    b. gives emergency aid at the scene of an accident
    c. performs cosmetic surgery to straighten a patient's nose
    d. provides well-baby care for a newborn
    e. treats a patient for a mild upper respiratory infection

5. When the parents of an 8-year-old boy were divorced, the father was awarded legal custody of the child. The father decided to send the boy to an aunt in California for the summer vacation. The aunt finds the boy's behavior rather strange and thinks he may have some emotional problems. She takes the child to a pediatrician who refers them to a psychiatrist. Before treating the child, the psychiatrist should have the consent of the
    a. child's mother
    b. child's father
    c. child's aunt
    d. child's mother and father
    e. California juvenile court

6. In nonemergency situations, operations may be extended if

    a. It is in the best interest of the spouse
    b. It is in the best interest of the surgeon
    c. It is considered good surgical practice

7. The legal consequences of treating a patient without valid consent can be a suit for

    a. assault and battery
    b. invasion of privacy
    c. professional negligence

8. Legal authorization for medical treatment can be given by

    a. a mentally competent delirious adult
    b. either parent in the case of separation or divorce
    c. a spouse of a competent adult
    d. an emancipated minor

ANSWERS TO EXERCISES

MATCHING

1. d
   e
   g
   b
   h
   i
   c

COMPLETION

1. greater; greater
2. fiduciary
3. *Caveat emptor*
4. material
5. Canterbury
6. assault; battery
7. negligence
8. implied
9. emancipated
10. custodial

QUIZ

1. a
2. d
3. d
4. c
5. b
6. c
7. a
8. d

6

Negligence

PERSONAL PRACTICE EXERCISES

PROGRAMMED REVIEW

Instructions:
Cover the words in the left-hand margin with a piece of paper. Read the material that follows, filling in the blanks before uncovering the answers. Study this section carefully before proceeding to the next exercise. If you have any questions, reread the corresponding portion of the chapter in your text.

tort	A tort is a civil wrong for which the wrongdoer is liable for damages to the injured party. The _____ of negligence is the failure to do something a reasonable person in the same or similar circumstances would have done, or doing something a
reasonable / similar	_____ person in the same or _____ circumstances would not have done.
negligence	In lawsuits alleging either personal negligence or professional _____, there
standards	are _____ to which defendants are held. In personal negligence cases, the
reasonable	defendant is held to the " _____ person" standard. In professional negligence
profession	cases, the defendant is held to the "reasonable member of the _____" standard.
physician	In a suit against a physician, the standard is a reasonable _____. In a suit
medical assistant	against a medical assistant, the standard is a reasonable _____ _____.
	When the physician-patient relationship is established, certain obligations are owed to the patient. Every physician is required to possess knowledge and skill of a
reasonable	reasonable physician and to exercise care, judgment, and skill of a _____ physician. A reasonable physician is an average physician when compared to other physicians of the same school and specialty in the same or similar circumstances.
physicians	The physician is compared to _____, not to podiatrists or dentists, or to
specialist	some other professionals. The _____, such as an orthopedist, is compared to another orthopedist, not to an internist or dermatologist.
physicians	The physician is obligated to the standard of care of other _____ in the same or in similar localities under like or similar circumstances. This is called the
locality	_____ rule. It means that the basis of comparison is like physicians in the
similar / locality	same or in a _____ community. The _____ rule is most often applied to suits involving general practitioners and family physicians. In the national standard, the basis of comparison is like physicians throughout the country. The national
standard	_____ of care is most often applied to specialists.
	The majority of lawsuits against physicians are based on the allegation of profes-
negligence / relation-ship / reasonable	sional _____. The plaintiff must prove that the physician-patient _____ did exist, thereby obligating the physician to use _____ care. He/she must

negligence **injury**	prove that the negligence injured the patient. He/she must prove that the _____ was the proximate cause of the injury. Negligence must result in _____ in order to be compensable.
expert **care**	Expert medical testimony is required for explaining complex medical data to the jury of laypeople. The usual qualification of the _____ medical witness is that he/she be from the same school and specialty as the defendant-physician. Another qualification of the expert medical witness is that he/she be knowledgeable about the standard of _____ practiced in the defendant's community.
res ipsa loquitur **negligence** **injury** **injury**	There is a type of professional negligence case in which the plaintiff does not need the testimony of an expert witness. These cases are based on the doctrine of *res ipsa loquitur*. The Latin translation of this doctrine is "the thing speaks for itself." The judge decides whether the case is to be tried on the doctrine of _____ _____ _____. The decision is based on the existence of three conditions. One condition is that an injury occurred that could not have occurred unless there was _____. Another condition is that the defendant-physician had control over the apparent cause of the _____. The third condition that must exist is that the patient could not have contributed to the _____.
thing **itself** **defendant** **expert** **doctrine**	In lawsuits tried under the doctrine of *res ipsa loquitur* (the _____ speaks for _____), the defendant-physician is presumed liable on the basis of circumstantial evidence. Therefore, the burden of proof automatically shifts to the _____, who must show why he/she should not be found liable. Also, the plaintiff's need for _____ medical testimony is eliminated. A foreign object unintentionally left in the body during surgery is the type of case most often tried on the basis of this _____.
Damages **injury** **damages** **nominal**	In the professional negligence lawsuit, there are three types of damages. _____ are the monetary compensations awarded to the injured party for _____ or for loss caused by another's legal wrongdoing. One type of damages is nominal _____. This is a token compensation awarded when the court wishes to recognize that an individual's legal right was violated, but that no actual loss was proved. The usual _____ damages is one dollar.
general **compensatory** **special**	The second type of damages is actual or compensatory damages. Compensation is awarded for proved injuries or losses. Compensation for physical impairment, pain and suffering, and loss of earnings are considered _____ damages. Another type of actual or _____ damages is special damages. Compensation for losses due to the negligence but not the direct consequence of the negligence constitutes _____ damages. An example of special damages would be additional medical expenses.
punitive / exemplary	The third type of damages is referred to as punitive or exemplary damages. Compensation awarded beyond actual damages as the wrongdoer's punishment for the reckless or malicious nature of the negligence is _____ or _____ damages.
damages	When a physician's negligence causes a patient's death, the patient's heirs may recover _____ in accordance with the wrongful death statutes. The purpose

wrongful	of these _____ death acts is to compensate the heirs for losses they incur as a result of the death, such as loss of financial support.
	Respondeat superior is a legal phrase used to express the liability of an employer for the wrongful acts of an employee. The English translation of *respondeat superior* is "let the master answer." Employers are liable for the _____ acts or omissions of employees when the negligence occurs within the course and scope of employment. The _____ of employment refers to the normal business/working day. The _____ or responsibility refers to the assigned duties and responsibilities of the employee. The _____-_____ is responsible for the acts of the allied health employee as long as these acts are within the course and _____ of his/her employment. The employee is also responsible for his/her own negligence.
negligent	
course	
scope	
physician-employer	
scope	
master	Hospitals are responsible for negligence of their employees under the doctrine of *respondeat superior* (let the _____ answer), unless the employee is a temporary "borrowed servant" of the physician. Physicians are responsible for the negligence of the "_____ servant." The situation most commonly covered by the "_____ servant" doctrine occurs in the operating room where surgeons use hospital employees to assist with surgical procedures.
borrowed	
borrowed	
physician	Private duty nurses are employees of persons hiring, firing, and paying their wages. Therefore, the _____ would not be liable for negligence of the private duty nurse under the doctrine of *respondeat superior*.

COMPLETION

Instructions:
Fill in the words or phrases that will correctly complete the following statements. The answer key appears at the end of this chapter.

1. A/An _____ is a civil wrong for which the wrongdoer is liable for damages to the wronged party.

2. In _____ negligence cases, the defendant is held to the "reasonable person" standard.

3. In professional negligence cases, the defendant is held to the "reasonable member of the _____" standard.

4. The three points that the plaintiff must prove in a professional negligence lawsuit are
    a.
    b.
    c.

5. _____ _____ means that the negligent act was the direct cause of the injury for which the plaintiff is claiming damages.

6. A/An _____ _____ is an individual who, through education and/or experience, has knowledge of matters that people lacking that education or experience do not have.

7. The English translation for the Latin term *res ipsa loquitur* is "the _____ speaks for _____."

8. The three categories of damages recognized by the law are
   a.
   b.
   c.

9. The English translation of the Latin term *respondeat superior* is "let the _____ answer."

QUIZ

Instructions:
Each item that follows consists of a stem, followed by four true or false phrases or statements. Determine whether each of the phrases or statements is true or false, and then respond according to the following code.

> **Select:**   A. if only 1, 2 and 3 are correct
> B. if only 1 and 3 are correct
> C. if only 2 and 4 are correct
> D. if only 4 is correct
> E. if all are correct

Write your code-letter answer in the margin. The answer key appears at the end of this chapter.

1. In a lawsuit alleging professional negligence, the physician-defendant is held to the professional negligence standard. This means the treatment provided by a
   1. reasonable person under the same or similar circumstances
   2. reasonable nurse under the same or similar circumstances
   3. reasonable member of the dental profession under the same or similar circumstances
   4. reasonable member of the same profession under the same or similar circumstances

2. In the professional negligence lawsuit, the plaintiff must prove the following points by a preponderance of evidence:
   1. existence of the physician-patient relationship
   2. failure of the physician to use reasonable care
   3. that the negligence injured the patient
   4. that the patient's condition contributed to the injury

3. An expert medical witness is qualified if he/she
   1. is from the same school and has several years experience
   2. is knowledgeable about community practices, if applicable
   3. lives in the same community as the defendant-physician
   4. is from the same specialty as the defendant-physician

4. The judge decides whether a case may be tried on the doctrine of *res ipsa loquitur* on the basis of the existence of the following
   1. an injury occurred that could not have occurred unless there was negligence
   2. the defendant-physician had control over the apparent cause of the injury
   3. the patient could not have contributed to his/her injury
   4. the patient had control over the apparent cause of the injury

5. The types of cases most often tried on the basis of the doctrine of *res ipsa loquitur* are ones in which
   1. a foreign object is unintentionally left in the body during surgery
   2. the patient is accidentally burned while anesthetized
   3. some part of the patient's healthy tissue is damaged during surgery on another part of his/her body
   4. the patient suffers an infection due to the use of unsterilized instruments

6. When a plaintiff can prove that he/she was injured by the defendant's negligence, the plaintiff may be entitled to actual or compensatory damages. This means
   1. token compensation awarded when the court wishes to recognize that the plaintiff's legal right was violated
   2. compensation for the consequences of the wrong, such as pain and suffering
   3. compensation awarded beyond actual damages as punishment to the wrongdoer for the reckless nature of the wrongdoing
   4. compensation awarded for losses, such as additional medical expenses

7. The legal phrase used to express the liability of an employer for the wrongful acts of the employee that most closely applies to the relationship of the physician/allied health employee is
   1. *stare decisis*
   2. *res judicata*
   3. *expressio unius exclusio alterius*
   4. *respondeat superior*

8. Under the doctrine of *respondeat superior*, the physician would be liable for the negligent actions or omissions of
   1. the medical assistant
   2. other physicians
   3. the hospital employee who is a temporary "borrowed servant"
   4. the private duty nurse

ANSWERS TO EXERCISES

COMPLETION

1. tort

2. personal

3. profession

4. a. that the physician owed the patient the standard of care
   b. that the physician was negligent
   c. that the physician's negligence was the proximate cause of the patient's injuries

5. proximate cause

6. expert witness

7. thing; itself

8. a. nominal
   b. actual or compensatory
   c. punitive or exemplary

9. master

QUIZ

1. D
2. A
3. C
4. A
5. E
6. C
7. D
8. B

7
Defenses to Professional Liability Suits

PERSONAL PRACTICE EXERCISES

PROGRAMMED REVIEW

Instructions:
Cover the words in the left-hand margin with a piece of paper. Read the material that follows, filling in the blanks before uncovering the answers. Study this section carefully before proceeding to the next exercise. If you have any questions, reread the corresponding portion of the chapter in your text.

documentation
liability

Well-kept medical records are important defenses to professional liability suits. Medical records serve two uses in lawsuits. They refresh the defendant's memory and provide documentation of care provided. Without accurate records to refresh the memory of the physician, the jury may equate loss of recollection with intentional concealment. Well-kept records reflecting adequate care serve as _____ and strengthen the defense to professional _____ suits.

well-kept
original / obliterate
correct
incorrect

Original entries in _____-_____ records should remain legible. To correct an _____ entry, the allied health professional must never _____ the error. To _____ a medical record, the allied health professional should draw a single line through the _____ entry and make a marginal note regarding by whom, why, and when the change was made. Correct information should be entered in chronological order.

denies
affirmative
injury
negligence

In the denial defense, the defendant _____ negligence and liability for the patient's alleged injury. In an _____ defense, the defendant presents new factual evidence to show that the patient's alleged _____ is due to some cause other than the _____ of the physician.

contributory
negligence
totally

One type of affirmative defense is contributory negligence. In _____ _____ the defendant claims that the patient's condition is at least partly, and sometimes _____, the patient's fault. Fault may be caused by the failure of the patient to follow the physician's instructions, which should always be documented in the medical record.

defense
res judicata

A technical _____ is based on the doctrine of *res judicata*. "The thing has been decided" is the translation of _____ _____. This defense means that once a case has been resolved on its merits, it cannot be tried again on the basis of the same evidence.

limitations / technical The statute of _____ is another _____ legal defense to professional
statute / law liability suits. Every state has a _____ of limitations, which is a _____
time limiting the amount of _____ in which an injured party can file a claim for
damages due to medical negligence. State statutes of limitations vary not only in
length _____, but also in ways of determining when the statutory period begins.

begins The more common ways of determining when the statutory period _____ are:
the (1) occurrence rule; (2) last treatment rule; (3) discovery rule; and (4) a
combination policy.

Many states follow the occurrence rule, which means that the statutory period
occurred begins the day the alleged negligence _____. A few states follow the
last treatment _____ _____ rule, which sets the beginning date of the statutory
stopped period as the day the physician _____ treating the patients. A significant
discovery rule number of states have adopted the _____ _____, which means that
discovered the statutory period begins the day the patient discovers or should have _____
the negligence. A combination policy establishes a maximum length of time within
which a suit must be brought on the basis of the occurrence rule and establishes a
shorter time for the discovery rule.

Almost all states recognize conditions tolling or extending statutory limitations
Tolling periods. _____ means interrupting. These conditions are fraud, confinement
preventing the patient from pursuing the case, and the presence of a foreign object
after surgery.

Statutory periods for filing breach of contract suits tend to be longer than periods for
liability filing professional _____ suits.

MATCHING

Instructions:
Match the terms in the left-hand column with the letter corresponding to the correct definitions or descriptions in the right-hand column. The answer key appears at the end of this chapter.

1. ___ toll   a. deception
   ___ fraud   b. exemption
   ___ statutory   c. interrupt
   ___ tortfeasor   d. wrongdoer
   ___ *res judicata*   e. to lessen
   ___ *res ipsa loquitur*   f. take for granted
                     g. pertains to a law enacted by a legislature
                     h. "let the master answer"
                     i. "the thing speaks for itself"
                     j. "the thing has been decided"

COMPLETION

Instructions:

Fill in the words or phrases that will correctly complete or respond to the following statements or questions. The answer key appears at the end of this chapter.

1. Two uses of medical records in professional liability suits are
   a.
   b.

2. Define contributory negligence

3. Technical defenses to professional liability suits are
   a.
   b.

4. Three conditions tolling statutory limitations periods are
   a.
   b.
   c.

5. The _____ rule means the statutory period begins the day the negligence occurred.

6. The _____ _____ rule means the statutory period begins the day the physician stopped treating the patient.

7. The _____ rule means the statutory period begins the day the patient discovers, or should have discovered, reason to suspect negligence.

ANSWERS TO EXERCISES

MATCHING

1. c
   a
   g
   d
   j
   i

COMPLETION

1. a. to refresh the defendant's memory
   b. to provide documentation of care provided
2. Contributory negligence is a defense to a professional liability suit. The defendant claims that the patient's condition is at least partly and sometimes totally the patient's fault, often due to the patient's failure to follow the physician's instructions.

3. a. *res judicata*
   b. statutes of limitations

4. a. fraud
   b. confinement preventing the patient from pursuing the case
   c. presence of a foreign object after surgery

5. occurrence

6. last treatment

7. discovery

8

Intentional Torts and Criminal Offenses

PERSONAL PRACTICE EXERCISES

PROGRAMMED REVIEW

Instructions:
Cover the words in the left-hand margin with a piece of paper. Read the material that follows, filling in the blanks before uncovering the answers. Study this section carefully before proceeding to the next exercise. If you have any questions, reread the corresponding portion of the chapter in your text.

torts
intentional
expert

An intentional tort is a deliberate violation of another person's legal right. Damages caused by intentional _____ are not usually covered by standard professional liability insurance. Ordinarily, actions considered to be _____ torts do not involve medical treatment, and neither plaintiffs nor defendants use _____ medical testimony to justify their positions.

intentional
assault
assault / battery

An example of an _____ tort is assault and battery. The use of physical contact and/or force without the victim's permission is _____ and battery. The threat of contact is _____ and the act of contact or force is _____.

duress
consent / duress
battery

Duress is an intentional tort. Coercion designed to make the victim do something against his/her will is _____. Duress invalidates consent, and a patient whose _____ was obtained through _____ may also sue for assault and _____.

tort
confidential

betrayal

Malicious betrayal of a professional secret is another intentional _____. The physician-patient relationship is a _____ one, and, except when required by law, physicians must refrain from discussing patients with any third parties. Malicious_____ of a professional secret could subject the physician to punitive damages, license revocation, and, in some states, criminal prosecution.

defamation

libel / slander

Defamation of character is an intentional tort. Injuring a person's name, reputation, or character by false and malicious statements is _____ of character. An untrue statement made orally is slander. Libel is an untrue written or broadcast statement. Truth is a defense to a charge of _____ or _____; but, it is wholly ineffective in a malicious betrayal of a professional secret action.

False imprisonment is the unlawful detention or restraint of an individual.

false

false imprisonment

imprisonment

Involuntary commitment of the patient to a hospital because of malice would be considered _____ imprisonment. If the physician fails to abide by statutory commitment procedures governing involuntary commitment of patients to mental hospitals or psychiatric wards, he/she could be charged with _____ _____. Detaining a person for any reason without the legal authority to do so could result in a false _____ charge.

intentional / Fraud

fraud
fraud
risks
unnecessary / fraud

Fraud is another example of an _____ tort. _____ is an act performed, or not performed, to intentionally and deliberately misrepresent or conceal the truth. The charge of _____ could be made for minimizing the patient's injuries or raising false hopes for recovery. The physician could commit _____ by concealing serious _____ inherent in a procedure or by advising the patient to have worthless or _____ surgery. Another example of _____ is misrepresenting a procedure before or after treatment. Concealing or misrepresenting your own or a colleague's mistake would be committing fraud.

fraudulent
unneeded
codes / dates

Medicaid, Medicare and many other insurance companies are prosecuting health care providers for a wide spectrum of _____ activities such as billing for services not rendered or for _____ procedures, using inappropriate _____ for billing, writing fraudulent diagnoses and altering _____ of services.

Undue influence
influence

undue influence

Undue influence is the improper swaying of another person in a way that destroys the person's freedom to act. _____ _____ is an intentional tort. The charge of undue _____ most commonly arises when elderly, senile, or mentally incompetent patients do something that materially enhances the health care provider's economic position. An example could be the situation in which an elderly patient leaves an allied health professional a substantial sum in a will. The allied health professional could be accused of _____ _____ by the patient's heirs.

Criminal
criminal

law / Criminal
state
evil

Criminal offenses rarely occur within the health care system. _____ offenses are acts specifically established and defined by law. A _____ offense is the commission of an act forbidden by law, or the omission of an act required by _____. _____ offenses are offenses against the state, and they are prosecuted by the _____. The two elements in a criminal offense are the act itself and an evil intent. The term _____ intent means that the person knew the act was unlawful but did it anyway.

misdemeanors
felonies

Criminal offenses are classified as misdemeanors or felonies. Lesser crimes with less serious penalties are classified as _____. More serious crimes with penalties including imprisonment for one or more years are called _____.

murder
murder
Second

An example of a criminal offense is _____, which is the unlawful killing with the intent to kill. First-degree murder is willful and deliberate _____. _____-degree murder is an unlawful killing but not one made with deliberation. The unlawful killing without malice or intent to kill, such as death due to gross negligence, is manslaughter.

Mercy killing

Euthanasia, _____ _____, and assisted suicide are forms of murder that are receiving wide attention now. At the present time, there are no clear cut

guidelines / cases	_____ and no consistency in the way the authorities handle _____. Assault and battery is another example of a criminal offense. The deliberate physical
assault	or sexual attack on a person or patient could result in the offense of _____
battery	and _____.
abuse	Domestic violence has been pushed to the forefront of national awareness in the past few years. Federal and state legislation defines child _____ as "mistreatment of
injury	a child by a parent or other responsible caretaker that causes _____ or harm or
risk / Neglect	puts the child at _____ of injury or harm." _____ is defined as failure to provide adequate food, clothing, shelter, or other basics for a child.
mandate	Child abuse laws _____ reporting of suspected cases and list individuals who
providers	are mandated as reporters, including health care _____. In most states a health
suspicion	care provider who in good faith reports _____ of child abuse is immune from
defamation	suit for negligence or _____ of character if the suspicion is not confirmed.
abuse	Although most states do not have laws that mandate the reporting of spouse _____, abuse of the elderly and abuse of dependent adults, this may change in the next few
severity	years as a result of the growing awareness of the frequency and _____ of domestic violence other than child abuse.
unlawful	Embezzlement is defined as the _____ taking of the property of another by a
robbery	party entrusted with the property. Embezzlement is different from _____ because there is no taking by use of force or fear. Employees who have embezzled
job	in one medical or dental office will frequently get another _____ in a health care office and embezzle again. A system of good internal controls and prosecution of the criminal is recommended.
	Each state and the federal government have enacted a number of statutes governing the performance of certain medical procedures. Practicing medicine without a
license	_____ is a statutory offense. Noncompliance with federal and state nar-
statutory	cotic legislation is a _____ offense. Another statutory offense is not reporting communicable diseases or cases of suspected child abuse. Disregarding procedures
statutory	regarding commitment of mentally ill patients is another example of a _____ offense.

COMPLETION

Instructions:
Fill in the words or phrases that will correctly complete the following statements. The answer key appears at the end of this chapter.

1. A/An _____ _____ is a deliberate violation of another's legal right.

2. _____ and _____ is the use of physical contact and/or force without the victim's permission.

3. Coercion designed to make the victim do something against his/her will is known as _____.

4. Defamation of _____ is injuring a person's name, reputation, or character by false and malicious statements.

5. The unlawful detention or restraint of someone can result in the charge of false _____.

6. _____ is an act performed—or not performed—to intentionally and deliberately misrepresent or conceal the truth.

7. The improper swaying of another in a way that destroys the person's freedom to act is known as _____ influence.

8. Criminal offenses consist of two elements: (1) the act itself; and (2) evil _____.

9. Unlawful killing without malice or intent to kill, such as death due to gross negligence, is known as _____.

10. An untrue and malicious oral statement injuring a person's name, reputation, or character is called _____.

QUIZ

Instructions:
Select and then circle the letter corresponding to the one best ending or response to each of the following statements or questions. The answer key appears at the end of this chapter.

1. The physician who uses physical contact and force to perform a procedure without the patient's permission could be charged with
   a. undue influence
   b. false imprisonment
   c. fraud or deceit
   d. assault and battery

2. The allied health professional who incorrectly reports that an unmarried woman is pregnant may be charged with:
   a. assault and battery
   b. undue influence
   c. fraud or deceit
   d. defamation of character

3. Criminal offenses are:
   a. not applicable to the medical industry
   b. offenses that commonly occur within the health care delivery system
   c. offenses against the state that are prosecuted by the state
   d. decided by a preponderance of evidence

4. An example of a criminal offense is murder. Murder is:
   a. the unlawful killing with the intent to kill
   b. first-degree when it is willful and deliberate
   c second-degree when it is malicious but without deliberation
   d. all of the above

5. Health care providers frequently refuse to press charges against an embezzler. The reasons for this reluctance are:
   a. the fact that it is seldom possible to recover fully from the embezzler
   b. the health care providers are not willing to admit that they are victims
   c. the criminal trial of an embezzler is a very long process
   d. all of the above

6. Dependent adults are:
   a. persons who are 65 years of age or older
   b. adults with physical and mental limitations that restrict their ability to protect their rights
   c. the nonemployed spouse in a marriage
   d. any nonminor seen by a physician

7. In the case of suspected child abuse, the duty of confidentiality is owed to the:
   a. state
   b. parents
   c. court
   d. child

ANSWERS TO EXERCISES

COMPLETION

1. intentional tort
2. assault, battery
3. duress
4. character
5. imprisonment
6. fraud
7. undue
8. intent
9. manslaughter
10. slander

QUIZ

1. d
2. d
3. c
4. d
5. d
6. b
7. d

9

Public Duties and Responsibilities

PERSONAL PRACTICE EXERCISES

PROGRAMMED REVIEW

Instructions:
Cover the words in the left-hand margin with a piece of paper. Read the material that follows, filling in the blanks before uncovering the answers. Study this section carefully before proceeding to the next exercise. If you have any questions, reread the corresponding portion of the chapter in your text.

obligations obligations statutes statute / duty	In addition to _____ to their individual patients, physicians have obligations to the states and communities in which they practice. Many of these _____ are established by a body of statutes known as public health _____. Remember that the physician's duty to comply with the _____ supersedes the _____ to keep patient information confidential.
Vital	All states collect vital statistics on their citizens. _____ statistics is the term covering the birth, death, marriage, and divorce records.
birth / birth physician filing / physician responsibility	Most states utilize the United States Standard Certificate of Live Births. When a _____ occurs in a hospital, the physician certifies that the _____ occurred and a hospital employee files it with the proper agency. When a birth occurs at home, the attending _____ is responsible for completing the form and _____ it with the proper agency. In the absence of a _____, the person in charge of the birth would assume this _____.
vital Death / statistic birth / death	Deaths are also a part of _____ statistics. Most states use the United States Certificate of _____ to report this vital _____. A special fetal death or stillbirth certificate, combining the relevant features of _____ and _____ certificates, has been adopted in many states.
vital statistic	The _____ _____ reports of birth and death are reports prepared as permanent records.
medical examiner death cause	There are many cases of death that must be reported to the _____ _____. The role of the medical examiner is to establish the cause of _____. In all states, the medical examiner has jurisdiction over any case in which a criminal or violent act is a suspected _____ of death. Most states also give the medical

jurisdiction
death

examiner _____ over: (1) death due to unknown cause; (2) cases in which the decedent was not attended by a physician at the time of _____; and (3) cases in which the physician was unable to establish a diagnosis before death occurred.

statutes
protect
reported
reported
health
statutes
report

Public health _____ require the reporting of certain infectious, contagious, or communicable disease to _____ the well-being of the citizens. State regulations determine those diseases that must be reported, how they are to be_____, and when they must be _____. Reporting regulations vary from state to state, and forms are available through most county _____ departments. One must become familiar with his/her own state _____, because failure to _____ may result in criminal prosecution and/or civil suit.

violence / law

Injuries caused by_____ must be immediately reported to the local _____ enforcement agency. The report should include the patient's name, his/her whereabouts, and the extent of his/her injuries.

child abuse

child abuse / liable

Cases of child abuse, suspected or confirmed, must be reported. Anyone making a "good faith" report of _____ _____ is immune from suit for negligence or defamation of character if the suspicion is not confirmed. A physician failing to report _____ _____ may be found _____ for negligence.

medical examiner
consent

daughter
sister

Autopsies require valid consent of the person with the first right to the body, unless the case falls under the jurisdiction of the _____ _____. Valid _____ of the first right to the body recognized by most states is in the following descending order: (1) surviving spouse, if a normal marital relationship existed at the time of death; (2) adult son or _____; (3) parent; and (4) brother or _____.

legal
critical
inaccurate
compromised

When specimens are obtained that might be significant in a _____ situation or a court case, the chain of custody of those specimens is of _____ importance. If the procedure is not properly followed or the paperwork is _____ or incomplete, the validity of the specimens is _____.

protect
preserved
evidence
authorities

When the victim of a crime is seen, whether in an emergency room or in a private office, it is necessary to obtain, preserve, and _____ the integrity of possible evidence. All specimens must be carefully obtained and _____ in a sealed bag. Complete identification must be placed with the piece of _____; all evidence must be held in a locked cabinet until delivered to the proper _____ and a receipt received.

statutes / laws
commitment

Another medicolegal subject is that of commitment of the mentally ill. Again, states vary in their _____. The physician must know and abide by the state _____ governing involuntary _____ of the mentally ill.

commitment

commitment/medical

Statutes governing involuntary _____, in most states, permit authorization of hospitalization only when there is recent, direct evidence that a person may be harmful to himself/herself or others. Medical certification attesting to the need for _____ is required. It is based on a recent _____ examination. The patient

committed	must be notified in advance that he/she is to be _____ and that he/she is entitled to legal counsel at appropriate times. A formal hearing must be held, with the decision being made by a judge, jury, or special committee.
medical	Most laws affecting the practice of medicine originate within each of the states. One area of _____ treatment is regulated primarily by federal law. This area concerns the prescribing, administering, and dispensing of drugs classified as
Controlled Substances	controlled substances. In 1970, the _____ _____ Act was passed.
federal / dispensing	This is a _____ law that regulates the manufacture, distribution, and _____ of narcotics and other dangerous drugs considered to have a high potential for
abuse	_____. The goal of this law is to create a closed system of distribution, one accessible only to legitimate handlers. The agency responsible for enforcing the law is the Drug Enforcement Administration, referred to as the DEA, which is in the United States Department of Justice. This Controlled Substances Act imposes
distributes / dispenses	jurisdiction over anyone who manufactures, _____, or _____
controlled	any _____ substances.
law	The _____ classifies the drugs it wishes to control into five schedules, Schedules I through V. Schedule I includes those that have a high potential for
abuse / medical	_____ and no accepted _____ use. Schedule II drugs have a high
potential / drugs	_____ for abuse, but have accepted medical uses. Schedule III _____
abuse	have a moderate potential for _____ and have many accepted medical uses. Schedule IV drugs have less potential for abuse than Schedule III drugs and have
medical / abuse	many _____ uses. Schedule V drugs have a potential for _____ and include many over-the-counter preparations .
dispenses	Any physician who administers, prescribes, or _____ any scheduled drug must
registration	register with the Drug Enforcement Administration. His/her assigned _____
registration	number must appear on all prescriptions and the _____ must be renewed
controlled	annually. If the physician administers or dispenses _____ substances
Drug	through more than one office, he/she must register each office with the _____ Enforcement Administration and notify the agency of any change of office address. A special registration permit must be obtained if the physician participates in
controlled	detoxification or drug treatment and uses _____ substances as a part of the
treatment	_____.
records	Special records must be kept regarding the dispensing of any narcotic drug. Special _____ must also be kept of the routine dispensing of any non-narcotic but controlled substances. The dispensing records must be kept for two years and may be inspected by the Drug Enforcement Administration within the U.S. Department
Justice	of _____. The following information must appear in the records: (1) the name and address of the patient; (2) the date the drug was given; (3) the quantity and character of the drug; and (4) the way in which it was dispensed.
Controlled	_____ substances must be kept locked and thefts must be reported immediately
Administration	to the local law enforcement agency and the Drug Enforcement _____.
criminal	Violation of the Controlled Substances Act is a _____ offense. The penalties
violations / penalties	for _____ range from fines to jail sentences. The _____ depend on the provision violated, the existence of criminal intent, and the frequency of offense.

crime
revoked

Recall that conviction of a _____ often results in the physician's license to practice being suspended or _____.

statutes
federal
laws

Most states have statutes regarding controlled substances. These _____ usually conform to and complement the _____ law. They require the physician to register with the state and to keep certain records. The state _____ may require the use of a special prescription form and may stipulate circumstances regarding oral prescriptions and the treatment of addicts. State laws set forth penalties for violations, and many prohibit physicians from self-prescribing or self-administering controlled substances.

blanks

record

behavior

There are many ways the allied health professional can prevent the illegal use of controlled substances. One precaution he/she can take is to see that the physician's bag is not accessible to the patients. He/she can see that prescription blanks are not left in unattended places. Prescription _____ can be obtained that have special features that minimize the possibility of alterations or that enhance the detection of thefts. Another precaution the allied health professional may take is to verify, with the patient's medical _____, any inquiry from the pharmacist regarding the authenticity of a prescription. He/she must always be alert to patient behavior that suggests a drug problem or an addiction and report this _____ to his/her employer before the patient is seen or treated.

COMPLETION

Instructions:

Fill in the words or phrases that will correctly complete the following statements or questions. The answer key appears at the end of this chapter.

1. The four vital statistics items reported are
   a.
   b.
   c.
   d.

2. With regard to the birth certificate, what is the responsibility of the physician when the birth occurs at home in his/her presence?

3. In descending order of authority, persons whose permission must be obtained before an autopsy may be performed are
   a.
   b.
   c.
   d.

4. Four causes of death that come under the jurisdiction of the medical examiner are
    a.
    b.
    c.
    d.

5. It is the responsibility of the physician who treats a patient for injury caused by violence to

6. To _____ a drug is to place it in the patient's body, such as an injection.

7. To _____ a drug is to give it to the patient in a container for later use.

8. To _____ a drug is to write an order for a drug.

9. Items of information that must be included in the dispensing records of controlled substances are
    a.
    b.
    c.

10. Conviction of a crime often results in the physician's license to practice being suspended or _____.

11. Dispensing records of controlled substances must be kept for a period of _____ years.

12. Five of the precautionary measures that the allied health professional may take to prevent illegal use of controlled drugs are:
    a.
    b.
    c.
    d.
    e.

QUIZ

Instructions:
Select and then circle the letter corresponding to the one best ending or response to each of the following statements or questions. The answer key appears at the end of this chapter.

1. The person with the property right and the right to consent to an autopsy in descending order is
    a. parent, brother or sister, spouse, adult son or daughter
    b. adult son, spouse, adult daughter, parent, brother
    c. spouse, parent, adult son or daughter, brother or sister
    d. spouse, adult son or daughter, parent, brother or sister
    e. brother or sister, spouse, parent, adult son or daughter

2. According to the Controlled Substances Act of 1970, heroin is classified as a controlled substance under
   a. Schedule I
   b. Schedule II
   c. Schedule III
   d. Schedule V

3. To dispense a drug means to
   a. place it directly in the patient's body
   b. give it to the patient in a container
   c. write an order for the drug
   d. call an order in for the drug

4. Dispensing records of controlled substances must be
   a. kept for two years and are subject to inspection by the Drug Enforcement Administration
   b. kept for three years and are subject to inspection by the Drug Enforcement Administration
   c. kept for four years and are subject to inspection by the Drug Enforcement Agency

5. The most closely regulated group of controlled substances is
   a. Schedule II
   b. Schedule III
   c. Schedule IV
   d. Schedule V

6. A physician must renew his/her registration with the federal Drug Enforcement Administration every
   a. six months
   b. year
   c. two years
   d. three years

7. The following must be reported to the appropriate state health department in all states
   a. case of confirmed gonorrhea
   b. case of suspected child abuse
   c. suspected homicide
   d. psychotic patient
   e. injury caused by assault with a knife

8. Schedule II drugs have
   a. high potential for abuse with no accepted medical uses
   b. high potential for abuse with accepted medical uses
   c. minimal potential for abuse, but no accepted medical use
   d. minimal potential for abuse and many accepted medical uses
   e. none of the above

9. A physician has a moderate supply of controlled substances on hand at the time of his/her retirement. He/she should
   a. give them to the county medical society
   b. give them to local law enforcement agencies
   c. offer them to the physician taking over the practice
   d. flush them down a municipal drain
   e. contact the Drug Enforcement Administration and follow its instructions

ANSWERS TO EXERCISES

COMPLETION

1. a births
   b. deaths
   c. marriages
   d. divorces

2. To collect the information and file the birth certificate

3. a. surviving spouse
   b. adult son or daughter
   c. parent
   d. brother or sister

4. a. when a criminal or violent act is a suspected cause
   b. death due to unknown causes
   c. when the deceased was not attended by a physician at the time of death or for a reasonable period of time preceding the death
   d. when the attending physician was unable to establish a diagnosis before the patient died

5. Telephone an immediate report to a local law enforcement agency; the report should include the patient's name, whereabouts, and the extent of injuries.

6. administer

7. dispense

8. prescribe

9. a. full name and address of the patient
   b. the quantity and character of the drug
   c. how it was dispensed

10. revoked

11. two

12. a. keep the physician's bag in a place inaccessible to any patients
    b. don't leave prescription blanks unattended
    c. obtain prescription blanks that have special features to minimize the possibility of alteration
    d. be alert and report to the physician any behavior that indicates the patient might have a drug problem or addiction
    e. verify all elements of a prescription by the medical record if the pharmacist should call the office to check the authenticity of a prescription

QUIZ

1. d
2. b
3. b
4. a
5. a
6. b
7. b
8. b
9. e

10

Patient Health Records

PERSONAL PRACTICE EXERCISES

PROGRAMMED REVIEW

Instructions:
Cover the words in the left-hand margin with a piece of paper. Read the material that follows, filling in the blanks before uncovering the answers. Study this section carefully before proceeding to the next exercise. If you have any questions, reread the corresponding portion of the chapter in your text.

medical **records** **aid** **legal** **peer** **educational**	Medical records have scientific, educational, financial, legal, and social purposes. The importance of _____ records cannot be overstated. They aid the physician in the practice of medicine. Patient health records contain a profile of the patient's health and they contain a data base. Patient health _____ are a link between the physician and others on the health care team. Therefore, they serve as an _____ to communication. Recall that medical records are a _____ document. Another purpose of medical records is in _____ review. They serve as a method of measuring the physician's competence. Medical records also have a scientific and _____ purpose because they are used in research and teaching.
financial **personal** **patient** **health record**	The medical record contains personal information, clinical information, and miscellaneous items of information. Medical records should not contain financial information. The financial information should be kept in the patient's _____ record. Data concerning the patient's personal and family medical background are a part of the _____ information of the medical record. Data concerning results of examinations, laboratory tests, and laboratory procedures are part of the clinical information. The clinical information also includes the physician's data, such as diagnosis, treatments, and prognosis. Miscellaneous information, such as consent forms, authorization forms, and correspondence, are a part of the _____ _____ _____.
	A question frequently comes up regarding ownership of the medical record. The physician owns the physician's office records. The clinic medical records belong to the clinic owner and hospital records belong to the hospital.
Patients **confidential**	_____ do not own the medical record, but they do have a right to have the information in the records released to authorized representatives, such as an attorney, another physician, and the insurance company. Recall that the patient does have the right to have the information in the confidential medical record kept _____.

lawsuit

Historically, the patient has been denied direct access to records. Records have been available to the patient's attorney upon instigation of a _____. There is now a trend, however, toward permitting direct access to the medical record by the patient.

retaining
retained

legal

There are many reasons for the retention of medical records. One reason for _____ the record, after the immediate need for treatment ceases, is to document the patient's health. Records should be _____ in order to serve as documentation of the patient's right to medical, insurance and legal benefits. Records are legal documents, so they should be retained for the doctor's _____ protection.

property

retained / limitations

retirement

destroy

A few states have statutes governing the length of time records must be retained. Most states, however, do not regulate or stipulate how long the physician must retain records, because the states consider the records to be private _____ of the physician. There are some retention guidelines to follow. The records should be _____ until all statutes of _____ have expired. Histories and other original records should be kept until the physician's retirement, if this is possible. Upon _____ of the physician, the record should be transferred to each patient's new physician or destroyed, if the name of the new physician is not available. The proper way to _____ a record is by shredding or burning it.

legal

entry

The following suggestions regarding keeping of the medical records pertain to the legal aspects of this very important topic. The medical record is a _____ document. The allied health professional should not make any entries unless his/her physician-employer authorizes him/her to do so. Every _____ should be dated and initialed. Personal opinions concerning a patient should not be entered in the medical record. Negative and normal findings, as well as positive findings, should be included in the record. Any notations, reports, or results of tests should be made in the record as soon as the event occurs.

single

Recall, from an earlier chapter, that there are proper ways to correct an error. Draw a _____ line through the incorrect entry. Make the correction in the margin, next to the entry, and in chronological order.

erase

change

Never obliterate, _____, or conceal the original entry. The allied health professional must never falsify a record. Never deliberately conceal a mistake, or _____ a record to reflect more favorably on anyone's actions.

action
record

The allied health professional should make a notation of a missed appointment and what action was taken. Telephone inquiries of a medical nature, along with the _____ taken, should be entered in the record. Any instructions given to the patient regarding health care should be documented in the record. Always _____ any prescription refills for the patient.

patient health

financial

Each time the allied health professional pulls a chart, and before he/she refiles it, he/she should check it for legibility and completeness. Medical and financial information should not be mixed in the _____ _____ record. Medical information belongs in the medical record and financial information belongs in the _____ record.

authorize
release
patient

authorized

original

The allied health professional must not reveal confidential information without written authorization by the patient. The patient may _____ the release of information, but not the record itself. The patient may authorize the _____ of information to insurance companies. With _____ authorization, the medical record may be transmitted to a new doctor in any one of several ways. The former doctor may send the new doctor a written summary of the patient's history and present condition if _____ by the patient. The former doctor may photocopy a part or all of the record and send it to the new doctor. The original record should be kept. Sending the _____ record is not a recommended practice.

subpoena duces tecum

subpoena
duces tecum

In an earlier chapter, the terms subpoena and _____ _____ _____ were covered. A court order requiring the recipient to appear at a certain time and place in order to testify is a _____. A court order to appear with the record is a *subpoena* _____ _____. The allied health professional could be served with a *subpoena duces tecum*. There are some customary procedures for responding to the service of a *subpoena duces tecum*. Before the server leaves the premises, the allied health professional should check to see that the subpoena includes the name and telephone number of the attorney issuing it and the court docket case number. He/she should check to see if the patient named in the subpoena was a patient of her/his physician-employer. If the allied health professional is given a copy of the subpoena, he/she should check to see if it is an exact duplicate of the one held by the server. Next, the allied health professional should

subpoena duces tecum

notify the physician that the _____ _____ _____ was served. He/she should also check with the court regarding the date and time of the trial. The allied health professional should then pull the subpoenaed records and review them to ensure completeness. If any medical reports are missing, they should be located and inserted in the record. The allied health professional should number the pages in the record and prepare a cover sheet itemizing its contents. Since this

legal / legal

record serves as _____ protection for the physician and is a _____ document, it must be stored in a locked cabinet or office safe. If the state law and the attorneys permit, the allied health professional should prepare to submit a photocopy of the original record. The allied health professional should keep the record in

security

her/his possession and maintain its _____ in court until he/she receives specific instructions from the judge or court officer. If the record is left in court, he/she should obtain a receipt for it. The next customary procedure is for the allied health professional to take the stand and introduce the record into evidence, if so required or ordered by the court.

subpoena

The attorney who issued the _____ is obligated to pay for the cost of reproducing and transporting the records to court.

COMPLETION

Instructions:
Fill in the words or phrases that will correctly complete the following statements. The answer key appears at the end of this chapter.

1. Five purposes for keeping medical records include
   a.
   b.
   c.
   d.
   e.

2. _____ _____ and _____ _____ are the two parts of a typical office medical record.

3. The records a physician initiates and maintains during the course of private practice belong to the _____.

4. The records initiated and maintained in a hospital belong to the _____.

5. The records initiated and maintained in a clinic belong to the _____.

6. _____ and _____ are two proper methods of destroying a record so that the patient's identity cannot be ascertained.

7. _____ means appear in court.

8. _____ _____ _____ means appear in court with the records.

QUIZ

Instructions:
Select, and then circle the letter corresponding to the one best ending or response to each of the following statements or questions. The answer key appears at the end of this chapter.

1. The records a physician initiates and maintains during the course of private office practice belong to the:
   a. patient, if over age 18
   b. parents, if patient is under age 18
   c. medical record clerk
   d. physician
   e. office

2. When the allied health professional is served a *subpoena duces tecum*, the costs of reproducing and transporting the records to court are borne by the:
   a. attorney who issued it
   b. patient
   c. physician
   d. allied health professional
   e. medical record clerk

3. Hospital records concerning patients admitted to or treated in the hospital by the physician are owned by the:
   a. patient
   b. medical record technician
   c. hospital
   d. physician
   e. physician and hospital

4. A patient with a large overdue bill asks the allied health professional to send his/her medical record to a new physician and gives the physician's name and address. He/she should:
   a. refuse to cooperate until the patient pays the physician-employer the amount owed
   b. tactfully refuse to comply with the request because the record belongs to the physician-employer
   c. send the original record to the new physician
   d. send the new physician photocopies of those portions of the medical record the physician-employer believes necessary
   e. give the patient a photocopy of the complete original record

5. A subpoena is a:
   a. legal document requiring the defendant in a lawsuit to appear in court at a certain time
   b. legal document requiring the appearance of a witness at a judicial proceeding
   c. legal brief describing the plaintiff's complaints
   d. document listing certain questions that must be answered by the defendant under oath

6. Authorization by the physician-employer for the allied health professional to make entries in the medical record:
   a. should be in written form
   b. should be in oral form
   c. should be in the job description
   d. is not necessary

7. To protect the patient's privacy and to create an atmosphere in which the patient will feel comfortable, the patient's medical history should be taken in:
   a. the reception room
   b. the presence of the relatives accompanying the patient
   c. the presence of friends accompanying the patient
   d. a private office or area

8. When the allied health professional is served a *subpoena duces tecum*, he/she should:
   a. review the subpoenaed records to make sure they are complete
   b. improve the legibility of the record
   c. make sure the patient referred to in the subpoena was actually seen by the physician
   d. add any items pertinent to the case before the record is submitted to court

ANSWERS TO EXERCISES

COMPLETION

1. a. an aid to practicing medicine
   b. an aid to communications
   c. a legal document
   d. peer review
   e. medical research and teaching

2. Personal information; clinical information

3. physician

4. hospital

5. clinic owners

6. Burning; shredding

7. Subpoena

8. *Subpoena duces tecum*

QUIZ

1. d
2. a
3. c
4. e
5. b
6. a
7. d
8. a

11

Employment Safety and Rights Law

PERSONAL PRACTICE EXERCISES

PROGRAMMED REVIEW

Instructions:
Cover the words in the left-hand margin with a piece of paper. Read the material that follows, filling in the blanks before uncovering the answers. Study this section carefully before proceeding to the next exercise. If you have any questions, reread the corresponding portion of the chapter in your text.

employment
welfare / safety

work / injury
safety

In the past, employers had a great deal of control over hiring and firing, conditions of _____, and the working environment. Certain laws have been passed in the past two decades to protect the health,_____ and _____ of employees Workers compensation laws provide compensation to the employee and dependents for _____- related illness and _____, provide rehabilitation, and encourage _____ in the workplace.

ensure
free
hazards / illness

The Occupational Safety and Health Act was passed in an attempt to _____ that employees are provided with a workplace that is _____ from recognized _____that cause serious injury or _____. OSHA regulations cover the physical workplace, materials, machinery, and equipment, as well as first aid, protective clothing and reporting requirements.

training / equipment
employees

Employers must comply with all applicable OSHA requirements, keep specific records, provide safety _____, require employees to wear safety _____ and discipline _____ for violations of safety rules.

standards
health/safety/clothing
hazardous

Employees must also comply with OSHA _____, follow employer safety and _____ rules, use _____ equipment and _____ when necessary, and report _____ conditions.

stricter / safety

Some states have imposed _____ health and _____ standards.

dangerous
poisonous
warning

Right-to-Know regulations give the health care employee and others the right to information about toxic substances, and the hazards of their use, as well as the protective equipment to use when handling _____ substances. Toxic and _____ chemicals, corrosive irritants, flammable materials, and carcinogens must have _____ labels. Material safety data sheets (MSDS) for these

employees

product/manufacturer

hazards / precautions

products must be made available to _____. The MSDS lists each ingredient in the _____. MSDS lists can be obtained from the _____ or prepared on site. In the case of a spill, the MSDS must be consulted to determine any _____ involved or necessary _____ that must be taken. Each incident requires documentation.

HIV / hepatitis B

semen/amniotic fluids

pleural

saliva

Bloodborne pathogens, such as _____ and _____ _____, are of particular concern to health care providers. Bloodborne pathogens include the following body fluids: _____, blood, _____ _____, vaginal secretions, synovial fluid, _____ fluid, pericardial fluid, cerebralspinal fluid, and _____.

According to regulations, employers must have:

employees

1. a list of all _____ who might be exposed to bloodborne diseases on either a regular or an occasional basis

exposure

2. a written _____ control plan

employee

3. one _____ in charge of OSHA compliance

protective

4. availability of _____ equipment and clothing

training

5. an employee _____ program in writing, and records of sessions and participants

biohazards

6. warning labels and signs denoting _____

identifying / disposing

housecleaning

decontamination

7. written guidelines for _____, containing, and _____ of medical waste in accordance with state and local laws; the method for _____ and _____, including laundry

guidelines / exposed

blood

exposure

8. written _____ for procedures to follow if an employee is _____ to _____ or other potentially infectious materials, as well as a policy for reporting incidents of _____ and maintaining records

evaluation

9. postexposure _____ procedures

free of charge

Employers must also offer hepatitis B vaccine _____ _____ _____ to every employee who can be reasonably anticipated to have contact with blood or other potentially infectious materials.

handled

diapers

syringes / dressings

laboratory cultures

Recent laws require that medical waste be _____ with special care. Medical waste of concern includes bandages; body specimens; _____; disposable needles, _____, scalpels and other instruments; _____; _____ _____ and radioactive materials.

puncture resistant

tracked

stricter

Medical waste must be separated from other trash. Infectious wastes may be incinerated by the facility, or must be placed in _____ _____ special or lead-lined containers and removed by a medical waste disposal company. It must be _____ from the health care facility to the final incinerator or landfill. Some states have passed laws that are _____ than the federal laws.

fair

There have been many recent cases in which employers have been successfully sued for wrongful termination/discharge; therefore, it is important to comply with all laws regarding _____ labor practices.

wage

equal pay / child

forty (40) / lieu

The Fair Labor Standards Act regulates the federal minimum _____, overtime compensation, _____ _____ requirements, _____ labor and recordkeeping requirements. Overtime for nonexempt employees is considered work exceeding _____ hours per week; time off may not be given in _____ of pay.

disability
dependent / Medicare
pensions

The Social Security Act provides retirement benefits, _____ benefits, _____ benefits, survivor benefits and _____, while the Employee Retirement Income Security Act regulates and protects _____.

discrimination

One of the primary laws governing the relations among employers, supervisors, and employees is Title VII of the Civil Rights Act of 1964. It makes _____ in the workplace illegal.

discriminatory/impact
not

Title VII covers both _____ treatment and discriminatory _____. A job requirement may inadvertently be discriminatory if it is _____ really necessary for the job.

discharge
compensation
color
national

Employers may not: fail to or refuse to hire; limit, segregate or classify; _____; or otherwise discriminate against an individual with respect to _____, conditions, or privileges of employment, because of race,_____ sex, religion, or _____ origin.

sexual
mental
parenthood

Some state and local statutes prohibit discrimination on the basis of _____ orientation, personal appearance, _____ health, mental retardation, marital status,_____and political affiliation.

old
single / born
weight
citizenship

Care must be taken in hiring practices. For example, the following questions cannot be asked on an application or in an interview. How _____are you? Are you _____ or married? Where were you _____? What is your religious affiliation? What is your maiden name? What is your height and _____? Have you ever been arrested? In which country do you possess _____?

women

illegal / harassment

Sexual harassment has always been a common problem in the workplace. It has typically been directed toward _____ since they have been in fewer supervisory or management positions and could not afford to lose their jobs. Sexual discrimination is _____ under Title VII of the Civil Rights Act. Sexual _____ is considered to be a form of sex discrimination.

sexual

verbal
implicitly
rejection

intimidating
offensive

Sexual harassment is defined as unwelcome _____ advances or requests for sexual favors. In the 1980s the EEOC broadened the definition of sexual harassment to include other _____ or physical conduct of a sexual nature when: (1) submission to such conduct is made either explicitly or _____ a term or condition of an individual's employment; (2) submission to or _____ of such conduct by an individual is used as a basis for employment decisions affecting such individual; or (3) such conduct has the purpose or effect of unreasonably interfering with an individual's work performance or creating an _____, hostile, or _____ working environment.

exchange
quid quo pro
sexual
hostile
creatively / effectively
jokes

The most common situation has been the demand by an employer or supervisor for sexual favors in _____ for job promotion or retention. This type of situation is called _____ _____ _____ which means "something for something" in Latin. Another type of _____ harassment is the creation of an environment that is intimidating, _____ or offensive which interferes with the individual's ability to perform _____ or _____. This situation is most often associated with sexually explicit or gender-demeaning _____, comments, or actions.

harassment **limit**	A program to eliminate sexual _____ from the workplace not only is required by law, but also is the most practical way to avoid or _____ damages if harassment should occur.
	Employers should implement a plan such as the following:
tolerated **gender**	1. Prepare a written policy stating that sexual harassment will not be _____. 2. Provide education for employees with examples of sexual and _____ harassment as well as gender discrimination.
reporting **investigation**	3. Develop a procedure for _____ incidents that ensures confidentiality. 4. Provide prompt, thorough and objective _____ of the situation. All those with information about the incident should be interviewed.
communicated	5. A determination should be made and the results _____ to the complainant, to the alleged harasser, and—as appropriate—to all others directly concerned.
gender	6. If sexual or _____ harassment is proven, there must be prompt and effective action. First, appropriate action must be taken against the harasser
communicated **further** **remedy**	and _____ to the complainant. Second, steps must be taken to prevent any _____ harassment. Third, appropriate action must be taken to _____ the complainant's loss, if any.
40	The Age Discrimination in Employment Act makes it illegal for employers to discriminate against workers _____ through 65 years of age.
affirmative **promote**	The Rehabilitation Act of 1973 requires the federal government as an employer to implement _____ hiring practices for individuals with disabilities. Private entities receiving federal funding must also hire and _____ disabled employees.
hiring / advancement **privileges** **recruitment / layoff** **fringe benefits**	The Americans with Disabilities Act (ADA) prohibits discrimination in all employment practices, including job application procedures, _____, firing, _____, compensation, training, and other terms, conditions, and _____ of employment. The Act applies to _____, advertising, tenure, _____, leave, _____ _____, and all related activities.
major **limit** **nonchronic** **mental AIDS**	This statute applies to individuals with _____ (as distinct from minor) impairments. These must be impairments that _____ major life activities. The law does not apply to individuals with minor _____ conditions of short duration. The statute also protects persons with a history of cancer in remission, or a person with a history of _____ illness, or a person with _____ or who is HIV positive.
unrelated **disability / privileges**	No employer is required to hire a disabled applicant if the reason is _____ to the disability and is pertinent to the employment. An employer must ensure that a qualified individual with a _____ has the same rights and _____ in employment as nondisabled applicants/employees. Reasonable accommodations must be made for the disabled employee.

Examples of Basic Accommodations

parking

1. Extra-wide _____ slots reserved for the disabled as close as possible to the entrance.

inclined

2. Gently _____ ramps or elevators.

doors

3. Easy to open _____, usually electric.

36 inches

4. Unobstructed hallways (pathways) with at least _____ of clearance.

5. Bathroom handrails and facilities designed for the handicapped.

lounge

6. Accessible _____, lunch room or cafeteria

7. Reception counters and other work areas that are low enough for a person in a

wheelchair

_____ (maximum height of 34 inches.)

ergonomically

While the above guidelines represent the basic examples, it is possible that an employee with a back disability might simply require an _____-designed

work area

chair or a _____ _____ that is higher than the usual counter height in order to eliminate bending; a receptionist with a neck disability might require a

headset

_____ for the telephone. An employee who is confined to a wheelchair or a

scooter

_____ may need an office that opens directly into a main hall or outside area.

A job offer may be conditioned on the results of a medical examination, provided

all

the exam is required for _____ entering employees in the same job category with or without disability, and that information obtained is handled according to

confidentiality

_____ requirements specified in the Act. The ADA does take safety issues into consideration. The law expressly permits employers to establish qualification standards that will exclude individuals who pose a significant risk to the health and safety of others if that risk cannot be lowered to an acceptable level by reasonable

accommodations

_____.

illegal

Individuals who are currently engaged in the _____ use of drugs are specifically excluded from the definition of a "qualified individual with a disability" protected by the ADA when an action is taken on the basis of their drug use.

The employment provisions of the ADA are enforced under the same procedures

sex / religious

now applicable to race, _____, national origin, and _____ discrimination under Title VII.

family

Federal and state laws require covered employers to provide up to 12 weeks per year of unpaid, job-protected leave to eligible employees for certain _____ and medical reasons.

Unpaid leave must be granted for any of the following reasons:

birth / adoption

1. to care for the employee's child after _____, or placement from _____ or foster care;

2. to care for the employee's spouse, son or daughter, or parent, who has a serious

health

_____ condition;

3. for a serious health condition that makes the employee unable to perform the

employee's

_____ job

immigration

The Immigration Reform and Control Act was the first major revision of _____ policy in the United States in decades. The basic purposes of the Act were to:

1. preserve jobs for those who are legally entitled to them (i.e., American citi-

aliens

zens and _____ who are authorized to work in this country);

2. prohibit employers with four or more employees from discriminating against any authorized individual in hiring, discharging, or recruiting

citizenship

because of national origin or _____ status.

MATCHING

Instructions:

Match the terms in the left-hand column with the letter corresponding to the correct definitions or descriptions in the right-hand column. The answer key appears at the end of this chapter. There may be more than one definition per term.

1. _____ Age Discrimination in Employment Act
2. _____ Americans With Disabilities Act
3. _____ bloodborne pathogens
4. _____ Civil Rights Act Title VII
5. _____ Employee Retirement Income Security Act
6. _____ Fair Labor Standards Act
7. _____ Family and Medical Leave Act
8. _____ immigration reform
9. _____ medical waste laws
10. _____ Occupational Safety and Health Act
11. _____ Rehabilitation Act of 1973
12. _____ right to know regulations
13. _____ workers compensation laws

a. to preserve jobs for those legally entitled to them
b. to care for an adopted baby
c. to protect the rights of individuals with impairments that limit major life activities.
d. to implement affirmative hiring practices for individuals with disabilities in the federal government and entities receiving federal funding
e. to provide medical care, compensation for disability or death and rehabilitation, as well as promote safety in the workplace
f. to provide a workplace that is free from recognized hazards that cause serious injury or death
g. to provide special handling for body specimens, diapers, dressings, needles, syringes and other wastes
h. to regulate minimum wage, overtime compensation, equal pay requirements and child labor
i. to regulate and protect pensions
j. to provide retirement benefits, disability benefits, dependent benefits, survivor benefits and Medicare
k. to prohibit discrimination due to gender or sexual harassment or due to an intimidating, hostile, or offensive working environment.
l. to prohibit discrimination against workers between 40 and 65 years of age
m. to provide employees and others with information about toxic substances, the hazards of their use, and methods of safe handling
n. to provide workers with guidelines for protection from the pathogens in semen, saliva, blood, amniotic and pleural fluids
o. to prohibit discrimination in employment based on sex, race, color, religion or national origin.
p. to require employers to make reasonable accommodations for disabled employees.
q. to protect the employment status of an employee who is on leave due to a serious health condition.

ESSAY

Instructions:
Respond to the following directions in writing. Doing so will reinforce the concepts and procedures present-ed in Chapter 11 of the text. The answer key appears at the end of this chapter of the workbook.

1. Identify three laws that protect employees' rights.

2. Describe the primary purpose(s) of the workers compensation laws.

3. Explain the responsibilities of both employer and employee under OSHA regulations.

4. Outline a procedure, in compliance with Title VII of the Civil Rights Act, to prevent sexual harassment in the workplace.

5. Explain "quid quo pro."

6. Explain the concept of a hostile environment in the workplace.

COMPLETION/MULTIPLE CHOICE

Instructions:
Select and then circle the letter corresponding to the one best ending or response to each of the following statements or questions. The answer key appears at the end of this chapter.

1. The legislation that implemented affirmative hiring practices for individuals with disabilities for employ-ment with the federal government and all entities that received federal funding was the
   a. Americans with Disabilities Act
   b. Civil Rights Act Title VII
   c. Fair Labor Standards Act
   d. Rehabilitation Act of 1973
   e. workers compensation laws

2. Common accommodations for disabled employees, under the Americans with Disabilities Act, include the following items *except*:
   a. building gently inclined ramps or elevators and easily opening doors, usually electric
   b. installing handrails in bathrooms and making lunch rooms or cafeterias easily accessible
   c. providing a telephone headset and ergonomically designed chair for an employee with a neck injury
   d. redesigning a five story building to increase all of the stairwells to 36 inches of clearance

3. Laws require careful disposal of hazardous medical wastes. All of the following are considered to be hazardous medical wastes *except*:
   a. audiometers
   b. bandages
   c. diapers
   d. syringes

4. When interviewing an applicant for a job, which of the following is an illegal topic?
   a. current place of employment
   b. education and training
   c. marital status
   d. professional credentials

5. The type of sexual harassment in which a supervisor or employer demands sexual favors in exchange for job promotion or retention is called:
   a. *pro bono*
   b. *quid pro quo*
   c. *res ipsa loquitur*
   d. tortfeasor

6. Right to know regulations provide health care workers with information about all of the following *except*:
   a. biodegradable cleaners
   b. carcinogens
   c. corrosive irritants
   d. flammable materials

7. If the personnel director of a radiology practice is interviewing an applicant for a position as a radiologic technologist, the following question is illegal:

   a. What languages can you speak, read or write?
   b. Have you ever been convicted of a crime?
   c. What was your maiden name?

8. Under Title VII of the federal Civil Rights Act, discrimination is prohibited on the basis of:

   a. sexual orientation
   b. personal appearance
   c. mental retardation
   d. national origin

TRUE AND FALSE

Instructions:
Determine whether each of the following phrases or statements is true or false and then respond by writing "T" or "F" in the margin. The answer key appears at the end of this chapter.

1. If a medical secretary makes the daily bank deposit during his/her lunch period, he/she is entitled to overtime pay if the employer permits the practice.

2. The Social Security Act of 1935 provides benefits for the survivors of a qualified individual.

3. Under the doctrine of *respondeat superior*, employers may be found liable for sexual harassment even if the offense was caused by an employee.

4. Media coverage concerning the presence of hazardous medical wastes on beaches and the fear of AIDS has prompted medical waste laws.

ANSWERS TO EXERCISES

MATCHING

1. l
2. c, p
3. n
4. k, o
5. i
6. h
7. b, q
8. a
9. g
10. f, g, m, n
11. d
12. m
13. e

ESSAY

1. Answers will vary but may include three of the following:
   a. Fair Labor Standards Act
   b. Civil Rights Act Title VII
   c. Age Discrimination in Employment Act
   d. Americans with Disabilities Act
   e. Family and Medical Leave Act
   f. Immigration Reform Act

2. The purpose of the legislation was to provide, without regard to fault, medical care and compensation for the employee and dependents for disability and death, to provide rehabilitation if necessary, to encourage employer interest in safety, and to promote safety in the workplace.

3. Employers must comply with all applicable OSHA standards, inform employees of OSHA requirements, keep specific records, compile and post an annual summary or work-related injuries and illnesses, provide safety training, require employees to wear safety equipment, and discipline employees for violations of safety rules.

   Employees must comply with OSHA standards, follow employer safety and health rules, use protective equipment and clothing when necessary, and report hazardous conditions. Employers may not discharge or discriminate against an employee for filing a complaint or testifying against an employer regarding OSHA violations.

4. Employers should implement a plan such as the following:

    a.   Prepare a written policy stating that sexual harassment will not be tolerated.

    b.   Provide education for employees with examples of sexual and gender harassment as well as gender discrimination.

    c.   Develop a procedure for reporting incidents that ensures confidentiality.

    d.   Provide prompt, thorough and objective investigation of the situation. All those with information about the incident should be interviewed.

    e.   A determination should be made and the results communicated to the complainant, to the alleged harasser, and—as appropriate—to all others directly concerned.

    f.   If sexual or gender harassment is proven, there must be prompt and effective action. First, appropriate action must be taken against the harasser and communicated to the complainant. Second, steps must be taken to prevent any further harassment. Third, appropriate action must be taken to remedy the complainant's loss, if any.

5. The most common situation has been the demand by an employer or supervisor for sexual favors in exchange for job promotion or retention. This type of situation is called *quid pro quo* which means "something for something" in Latin.

6. Another type of sexual harassment is the creation of an environment that is intimidating, hostile or offensive which interferes with the individual's ability to perform creatively or effectively. This situation is most often associated with sexually explicit or gender-demeaning jokes, comments, or actions.

COMPLETION/MULTIPLE CHOICE

1. d
2. d
3. a
4. c
5. b
6. a
7. c
8. d

TRUE AND FALSE

1. T
2. T
3. T
4. T

12

Consumer Protection Laws

PERSONAL PRACTICE EXERCISES

PROGRAMMED REVIEW

Instructions:
Cover the words in the left-hand margin with a piece of paper. Read the material that follows, filling in the blanks before uncovering the answers. Study this section carefully before proceeding to the next exercise. If you have any questions, reread the corresponding portion of the chapter in your text.

credit / collections
granting
debts / consumers
discrimination / harassment

Careful management of the business side of health care—including a positive philosophy and well-defined _____ and _____ procedures—is essential. A number of laws govern the _____ of credit and the practices concerned with collection of _____. Most of the legislation was designed to protect _____ from _____ and _____. It is essential to be familiar with these federal laws as well as individual state laws.

granting
race
age
public assistance

The Equal Credit Opportunity Act of 1977 prohibits discrimination in _____ credit. Individuals cannot be discriminated against because of color, _____, national origin, sex, religion, marital status, or _____. It is also illegal to deny credit because a person is receiving _____ _____ or has sought protection under bankruptcy laws.

correct
notified

specific

The purpose of the Fair Credit Reporting Act of 1971 is to allow persons to see and _____ their credit reports. If credit is denied to a patient based on a negative credit report from a credit reporting agency, the patient must be _____ and given the name and address of the agency. It is not necessary to give the patient the _____ information.

notified / missed
complex / finance

The Council on Ethical and Judicial Affairs of the AMA considers the following fees ethical if the patient is _____ in advance: fees for _____ appointments, fees for_____ insurance forms, and interest or _____charges.

written
one year

prior

The statute of frauds specifies which contracts must be _____ in order to be enforceable. If a contract is going to take more than _____ _____ to complete, or if a third party agrees to be responsible for the debts of another, it must be in writing _____ to treatment.

obstetrics
four / bilateral

written
interest

Some health care costs such as surgery, orthodontia, physical therapy, fertility proce-dures and _____ commonly involve an installment payment plan for patients. If there will be more than _____ payments and there is a _____ agreement, Regulation Z of the Consumer Protection Act of 1969 requires that a _____ truth in lending statement must be completed. It does not make any difference whether the doctor is charging _____.

legal
collect

The statute of limitations indicates the length of time in which _____ action can be taken to _____ a debt.

consumer
unfair / abusive
threats

One section of the Fair Debt Collections Protection Act (FDCPA) of 1978 protects the _____ against harassment caused by the creditor: using deceptive or _____ methods; using _____ or vulgar language; making threats that legally cannot be carried out; or making _____ of action that the creditor does not really intend to pursue.

once
reasonable / privacy
invasion / defamation

Patient/debtors cannot be contacted more often than _____ a week, only during _____ hours, and their _____ must be protected. Violation of the FDCPA can result in suits based on _____ of privacy, _____ of character, or other torts.

small
claims
evidence
witnesses
ruling
property

Overdue accounts that do not exceed a specific amount may be taken to _____ _____ court; a lawsuit would have to be filed in Superior Court for larger debts. The defendant/debtor is served with a summons. Each party brings _____ and _____ to court; the judge questions each party, reviews the evidence, and makes a _____. If the plaintiff wins a judgment, there is a legal right to garnish wages, bank accounts, and personal or real _____.

attorney
lien
paid
compromise/settle-
   ment / adverse

The federal Wage Garnishment Law of 1970 allows creditors to garnish or attach the debtor's wages and property. When services have been rendered to a patient who has obtained the services of an _____, and a claim is made against another person for causing the patient's injury, a _____ can be executed. The lien ensures that the doctor or facility will be _____ from any sums received by any _____ or _____ that the patient may obtain from the _____ party.

bankruptcy
claim
relief / protection
distributing / fair

Bankruptcy is a special consideration when dealing with accounts receivable. Once an office/creditor is notified that a patient/debtor has filed for protection under the _____ laws, all routine collection procedures must cease. The creditor may file a _____ with the bankruptcy court. The purpose of the bankruptcy laws is to provide _____ and _____ for the insolvent debtor, while _____ the debtor's assets in an equitable or _____ manner among the creditors.

contempt

A creditor can be fined for _____ of court for failure to comply with the bankruptcy laws.

spouse / relative

When a patient is deceased and there is still an outstanding bill, the statement of the account should never be sent to the _____ or a _____ unless there is a written agreement that that person is responsible for the debts of the deceased. After

decent / estate	a _____ interval, a statement should be sent to the _____ of the
executor	decedent in care of the spouse or next of kin. If the administrator or _____
Probate	of the estate is unknown, a request may be sent to the _____ Department of
	the Superior Court in the county in which the estate will be settled.
credit	Successful management of the financial aspect of the health care receivables
	practice requires a carefully developed _____ and collections policy that
	conforms to all federal and state consumer laws.

ESSAY

Instructions:
Respond to the following directions in writing. Doing so will reinforce the concepts and procedures present-ed in Chapter 12 of the text. The answer key appears at the end of this chapter of the workbook.

1. Explain the concept of professional courtesy.

2. List the types of discrimination that is prohibited by the Equal Credit Opportunity Act of 1977.

3. Identify the purpose of Regulation Z of the Consumer Protection Act of 1969.

4. List three practices that are prohibited by the Fair Debt Collection Practices Act of 1978.
   a.
   b.
   c.

5. Explain the significance of the following in relation to the collection of debts:
   a. garnishment
   b. bankruptcy
   c. liens
   d. statute of limitations
   e. claims against estates

MATCHING

Instructions:

Match the terms in the left-hand column with he letter corresponding to the correct definitions or descriptions in the right-hand column. The answer key appears at the end of this chapter. There may be more than one definition per term.

1. ____ bankruptcy
2. ____ estate
3. ____ statute of frauds
4. ____ garnish
5. ____ lien
6. ____ statute of limitations
7. ____ professional courtesy

a. an encumbrance upon a property to satisfy or protect a claim for payment of a debt
b. the length of time in which legal action can be taken to collect a debt
c. to attach property of a debtor, held by a third party, in order to obtain payment
d. laws that specify which contracts must be written in order to be enforceable
e. a discount or waiver of fees given to specific types of patients
f. laws that provide relief and protection to debtors and provide a fair method of distribution of assets to creditors
g. the interest in property of an individual at the time of death

---

ANSWERS TO EXERCISES

ESSAY

1. Professional courtesy is actually a discount or waiver of fees given to individuals or specific types of patients. Traditionally, physicians have treated other physicians and their family members without charging a fee. This courtesy is commonly extended to members of the clergy and their family members as well as related health care providers who are employed in the doctor's office, offices of associates, or the hospital, such as pharmacists, lab technicians, medical assistants, nurses, x-ray technicians, dental hygienists, and ophthalmology assistants.

2. The law prohibits discrimination based on race, color, national origin, age, sex, marital status or religion; in addition, persons who receive public assistance or those who have exercised their rights under consumer credit laws cannot be discriminated against.

3. The Truth in Lending Act, or Regulation Z of the Consumer Protection Act of 1969, requires that there be a written agreement for payment of fees if: (a) there is bilateral agreement; and (b) the fee is to be paid in more than four installments. It does not matter whether interest is charged; a truth in lending statement must be prepared.

4. When pursuing collection of past due accounts, it is important that there is no misrepresentation, harassment or threats. Patients cannot be contacted more frequently than once a week, only during reasonable hours, and their privacy must be protected. One section of the Act protects the consumer against harassment caused by the creditor using deceptive or unfair methods, using abusive or vulgar language or making threats that cannot be carried out legally or that the creditor does not really intend to pursue.

5. a. **Garnishment.** Under this law, creditors are allowed to attach a debtor's wages and property. The amount of employee earnings that may be withheld for garnishment in any workweek or pay period is limited.

   b. **Bankruptcy.** Federal bankruptcy laws were designed to accomplish two main goals. The first is to provide relief and protection to debtors who have become insolvent—incapable of paying debts. The second goal is to provide a fair method of distributing a debtor's assets among all creditors.

   c. **Liens.** A lien is an encumbrance upon property to satisfy or protect a claim for payment of a debt. When services are being rendered to a patient who has obtained the services of an attorney, and a claim is made against another person for causing the patient's injury, a lien can be executed.

   d. **Statute of Limitations.** The statute of limitations indicates the length of time in which legal action can be taken to collect a debt or pursue some other course of action. The time limit is not the same in each state, nor is it always the same for oral and written contracts.

   e. **Claims Against Estates.** Statements for bills owed by a deceased patient need to be sent, after a decent interval, to the estate of the decedent in care of the spouse or next of kin. The statement of account may not be sent to a relative unless there is a written agreement indicating that the relative is responsible for the debts of the deceased. A request may be sent to the Probate Department of the Superior Court in the county in which the estate will be settled if the name of the responsible relative, the executor, or the administrator of the estate is unknown. There will be a specific time limit to file a claim against an estate.

MATCHING

1. f
2. g
3. d
4. c
5. a
6. b
7. e

13

Litigation and Other Means of Preventing and Resolving Conflict

PERSONAL PRACTICE EXERCISES

PROGRAMMED REVIEW

Instructions:
Cover the words in the left-hand margin with a piece of paper. Read the material that follows, filling in the blanks before uncovering the answers. Study this section carefully before proceeding to the next exercise. If you have any questions, reread the corresponding portion of the chapter in your text.

increase

providers / dramatic

optimistic

As discussed in Chapter 1, An Introduction to Law, there are many reasons for the _____ in lawsuits against health care professionals. The media has had a significant effect on the perceptions of the American public about health care and health care _____. Media coverage tends to display the most _____ and/or traumatic news items. The result of this type of coverage is an unrealistically _____ view of the outcome of surgery and of the "magic bullet" effect of drugs, and an unnecessarily negative view of members of the health care field.

rapport

welfare / patient

long

staff

critical / failure

uncaring

unprofessional

The underlying cause of many cases of litigation is the breakdown of the _____ between health care provider and patient. A lack of empathy or understanding of another's thoughts or feelings, or the belief that the health care provider lacks genuine concern for the _____ of the _____, are important factors in triggering complaints, dissatisfaction, and lawsuits. The destruction of rapport can be caused by many things, including a _____ wait in the reception room followed by a long, cold wait in the exam room. The attitude of the doctor and the _____ (staff usually pick up the tone for the facility from the doctor or doctors in charge) is of _____ importance to the success or _____ of the professional relationship. Offices that are too cold and _____ alienate patients; offices that are too casual or _____ also create problems in the health care relationship.

lawsuits

outcome

monetary

The increase in specialization since World War II has created an obstacle in the need for rapport. Fees for services rendered are frequently a cause for patient dissatisfaction and subsequent _____. It is not necessarily the fee charged that causes the problem, but the fact that patients and their families equate the fee with the result or _____ of the services rendered. Another problem is the fact that patients do not know how to discuss and do not discuss the _____ aspect of service with the doctor.

frequently

The current health insurance situation has created its own problems: when contracts are renegotiated or jobs changed, health care providers are also _____ changed.

providers

If employees want the benefit of their employer's insurance coverage, they must choose new health care _____. Patients become angry. Frequently, the object of the patient's anger is the union or the employer, but the target of that

anger

_____ may be the health care provider. The fact that society has become suit happy and blame oriented are facts that cannot be overlooked.

support

All health care providers, associates, assistants and _____ personnel must practice preventive procedures in order to reduce their individual and collective exposure to litigation.

hospitals

One preventative measure that has been mandated for _____ for many years is quality assurance and risk management. The goal of QA/RM has been to provide quality patient care. The goal of offices, clinics and other ambulatory facilities is

quality
resolving

the same: to provide _____ patient care. Quality assurance is the activity of identifying and _____ problems in patient care; it involves ongoing monitoring, evaluation and improvement of care. Risk management involves efforts to

prevent / emotional

_____ physical and _____ injury to the patients, staff, and visitors, and to protect the financial assets of the organization by preventing those events that are

liability

most likely to lead to _____. Poor quality creates a risk and is likely to lead to liability.

sensitivity

Some common issues for risk management are appointment delays, lack of _____ to patient concerns, unsafe facilities, treatment errors, specimen collection and

labeling

_____ errors, and lack of documentation.

significant

There is no doubt that each member of the health care team plays a _____ role in the care given to the patient and in the overall feeling of confidence and satisfaction

breakdown
respect

of a patient, or in the _____ in communication, dissatisfaction of the patient, and eventually the loss of rapport and _____ of that patient and possibly the eventual initiation of a lawsuit.

preventing

The following general preventative guidelines have been selected to assist associate, assistant and support personnel in _____ litigation involving themselves and their employers. There are only six listed; all other points seem to fall into one of the categories listed below:

genuine

1. Always demonstrate a feeling of _____ concern for the welfare of all patients.

respect

2. Always _____ the confidentiality of the patient-doctor relationship.

scope

3. Never go beyond the _____ and training of your field.

4. Always obey federal and state laws as well as local ordinances. Do not commit a crime or be an accomplice before or after the fact.

procedures

5. Conscientiously follow the _____ designed to provide the best of care, and facilitate understanding between health care provider and patient. Be sure that your patient feels free to ask questions.

education

6. Keep current on the changes in your field. Continuing _____ is essential in health care.

MATCHING

Instructions:
Match the items in the left-hand column with the letter corresponding to the correct definitions or descriptions in the right-hand column. The answer key appears at the end of this chapter.

1. ___ complaint
   ___ deposition
   ___ interrogatory
   ___ pleadings
   ___ pretrial discovery
   ___ summons

   a. defendant's written response to the allegations presented in the plaintiff's complaint
   b. legal notice issued under authority of a court that requires the recipient to appear as witness at a judicial proceeding
   c. legal document that notifies a party he/she is the defendant in a lawsuit and requires him/her to appear in a certain court at a certain date and time
   d. oral questions and answers given under oath during pretrial discovery
   e. plaintiff's written statement of allegations against the defendant
   f. phase in the litigation process to uncover all relevant evidence
   g. written document that identifies issue(s) in dispute
   h. written list of assertions that one party asks the other to admit or deny
   i. written questions served by one litigant on the other

2. ___ appellate court
   ___ arbitration board
   ___ board of medical examiners
   ___ joint screening panel
   ___ trial court

   a. administrative agency empowered by the legislature to make legally enforceable rules governing the medical profession
   b. a review body composed of attorneys and physicians that studies the merits of a patient's claim and then advises whether a suit should be pursued
   c. a body in the state court system that has final authority on all matters not falling under the jurisdiction of the federal system
   d. United States Department of Justice
   e. lowest level of the state court system
   f. an out-of-court substitute for the litigation process (Decisions of this body are considered final, binding and enforceable by the courts.)
   g. a body that reviews trial court decisions when losing sides dispute a question of law
   h. specialty court of the federal system that has jurisdiction on all tax matters

COMPLETION/ESSAY

Instructions:
Respond to the following directions in writing. Doing so will reinforce the concepts and procedures present-ed in Chapter 13 of the text. The answer key appears at the end of this chapter of the workbook.

1. Identify and define the four phases of the litigation process.
   a.
   b.
   c.
   d.

2. List the procedures that may be applied during a pretrial discovery phase to gather information.

3. Explain the concept of quality assurance/risk management in health care facilities.

4. List and explain the six preventative measures identified in this text.
   a.
   b.
   c.
   d.
   e.
   f.

QUIZ

Instructions:
Select and then circle the letter corresponding to the one best ending or response to each of the following statements or questions. The answer key appears at the end of this chapter.

1. The body that reviews a trial court's decision when the losing side disputes a question of law is the
   a. appellate court
   b. board of medical examiners
   c. district court
   d. municipal court
   e. trial court

2. The four phases of the litigation process are:
   a. complaint, answer, response, reply
   b. deposition, jury selection, trial decision
   c. pleadings, pretrial, trial, appeal
   d. summons, trial decision, appeal
   e. None of the above.

3. The legal notice to a defendant in a lawsuit that requires his/her appearance in court at a certain time and place is the
   a. complaint
   b. lawsuit
   c. request for admissions
   d. subpoena
   e. summons

4. The sum total of answers made under oath by a witness in response to oral questions which are recorded by a court reporter is called a/an
   a. answer
   b. deposition
   c. interrogatory
   d. pretrial conference
   e. request for admissions

5. In the litigation process for civil law disputes, the written statement of allegations, grievances, and demands for compensation is known as the:
   a. complaint
   b. declaration
   c. additur
   d. response

6. Joint screening panels
   a. are a substitute for judicial proceedings
   b. attempt to eliminate claims without merit
   c. follow the same proceedings as are followed in a courtroom

7. The primary goal of quality assurance in health care facilities is
   a. to abide by requirements of the federal legislation
   b. to provide quality health care for patients
   c. to lower the cost of dental and medical care

ANSWERS TO EXERCISES

MATCHING

1. e
   d
   i
   g
   f
   c

2. g
   f
   a
   b
   e

COMPLETION/ESSAY

1. a. **Pleadings Phase.** The first phase of the suit is called the *pleadings* phase. The pleadings consist primarily of three legal documents designed to identify the controversial or disputed issues to be decided during trial. Only material relevant to issues described in the pleadings may be presented during trial. The pleadings usually consist of the *complaint*, the *answer*, and the *reply*.

    b. **Pretrial Discovery Phase.** The next phase in the litigation process is called the pretrial discovery phase. The main purpose of this period is to permit the parties to uncover all relevant information before trial. Pretrial discovery helps to ensure that the dispute is settled fairly and on the issues rather than on the ability of one litigant to surprise the other with concealed evidence.

    c. **Trial Phase.** The purpose of the trial is to hear the case in a neutral environment and to achieve a just settlement to the dispute. During the trial, the judge acts as a referee, so to speak, to ensure that both sides proceed in a fair, legally required manner. At any time in the litigation process, the parties are free to settle the matter among themselves and are often encouraged to do so.

    d. **Appeals Phase.** After a verdict has been declared, the losing side may appeal the decision to a higher court. However, one does not have an automatic right to a review by an appellate court. Appellate court reviews are granted only when the evidence suggests the strong possibility of error, injustice or impropriety during the trial court proceedings. The appeal must be based on an issue of law, rather than on the jury's decision concerning a fact or facts.

2. During the pretrial discovery phase, each party has the right to obtain information through one or more of the following procedures:

    a. **Interrogatories.** An interrogatory is a list of written questions prepared by one litigant and served on the other. The questions must be answered in writing and under oath.

    b. **Depositions.** A deposition is a statement made under oath by a witness or potential witness in a question and answer form. The questions are posed by an attorney and the responses of the witness are recorded verbatim by a court reporter who transcribes the proceeding.

    c. **Court orders.** A court order is a direction or instruction by the court for one party to produce documents or other objects for inspection and duplication by the other party. A court may also order an injured party to submit to a physical and/or mental examination when the party's condition is in dispute.

    d. **Requests for admissions.** Requests for admissions are written lists of assertions that one party asks the other to admit or deny.

3. **Quality assurance** is the activity of identifying and resolving problems in patient care; it involves ongoing monitoring, evaluation, and improvement of care. **Risk management** involves efforts to prevent physical and emotional injury to the patients, staff, and visitors, and to protect the financial assets of the organization by preventing those events that are most likely to lead to liability.

4. The six preventative measures are:

    a. Always demonstrate a feeling of genuine concern for the welfare of all patients. You owe each and every patient a duty of courtesy, consideration, respect and decent treatment. Always use tact and sensitivity when dealing with patients . . . and associates!

    b. Always respect the confidentiality of the patient-doctor relationship. Be careful about when and where you discuss patient matters in the office; you *never* discuss them outside the office.

    c. Never go beyond the scope and training of your field. Do not practice medicine or dentistry. Do not perform procedures that you are not confident or competent in performing. Don't hesitate to ask for assistance or declare that you have not been trained in a specific procedure.

    d. Always obey federal and state laws as well as local ordinances. Do not commit a crime or be an accomplice before or after the fact.

e. Conscientiously follow the procedures designed to provide the best of care and to facilitate understanding between health care provider and patient. Obtain informed consent, explain procedures, follow up thoroughly, and document carefully. Make sure that the patient understands the diagnosis or condition, the procedure, any instructions, and the reasons for each. Be sure that your patient feels free to ask questions.

f. Keep current on the changes in your field. Continuing education is essential in health care.

QUIZ

1. a
2. c
3. e
4. b
5. a
6. b
7. b

14

Medical Ethics and Bioethical Issues

PERSONAL PRACTICE EXERCISES

PROGRAMMED REVIEW

Instructions:
Cover the words in the left-hand margin with a piece of paper. Read the material that follows, filling in the blanks before uncovering the answers. Study this section carefully before proceeding to the next exercise. If you have any questions, reread the corresponding portion of the chapter in your text.

welfare
physician

American Medical Association Judicial Council opinions are based on certain ethical standards that have remained constant through time: (1) the paramount importance of the individual patient's _____, (2) the right of patients to choose their _____, and (3) the right of physicians to choose their patients.

scarce / benefit
quality

treatment
arbitrary
priority

Five factors relating to health care need should be considered when allocating organs or other _____ resources. The factors are: (1) the likelihood of _____ to the patient, (2) the impact of treatment in improving the _____ of the patient's life, (3) the duration of benefit, (4) the urgency of the patient's condition (i.e., how close is the patient to death), and in some cases (5) the amount of resources required for successful _____. The criteria are not to be applied in an _____ manner nor one criterion given precedence over the others and allowed to serve as a _____ principle.

pay
social
diseases
medical

Factors that are considered ethically unacceptable in allocating scarce resources are (1) ability to _____, (2) past use of resources, (3) contribution of the patient to society (_____ worth), (4) perceived obstacles to treatment (patients with multiple _____ or language barriers, alcohol and drug abusers, the indigent, the uneducated), and (5) contribution of the patient to his/her own _____ condition.

organs

Geographical priorities in the allocation of organs should be prohibited except when transportation of _____ would threaten their suitability for transplantation.

organs

ethical

Retrieval and transplantation of the _____ of an anencephalic infant is ethically permissible in accordance with determination of death guidelines. The degree to which the decision to have an abortion might be influenced by the decision to donate the postmortem tissue of the fetus is the primary _____ concern. There

abortion

payment
benefit

are several guidelines to be followed in this case: The decision to have an _____ must be made before any discussion of the use of fetal tissue is discussed. There is no _____ for the tissue, and the donor may not choose the recipient. The health care personnel involved in the abortion may not _____ from the tissue transplantation. There must be informed consent of both donor and recipient.

advances
insemination
womb

The concept of the the family has changed drastically in the past decade. Recent technological _____ have made it possible to achieve parenthood through in-vitro fertilization, GIFT (gamete intrafallopian transfer), artificial _____, and through the means of a surrogate _____. Couples may obtain donor eggs or donor sperm, if needed or desired.

genetic
prenatal

If there is a high risk of having a child with a _____ disease, it is possible to choose not to reproduce, to accept the risk, to undergo _____ diagnosis and abort an affected fetus, to use one of the artificial reproductive technologies, or to adopt a child.

prohibit
artificial

rights
ensure
opposed

Professional ethics do not _____ artificial human insemination. The informed consent of the woman seeking _____ insemination and her husband is necessary. A child conceived and born through Artificial Insemination Homologous (AIH) has the same legal _____ as a child conceived and born naturally. Extra precautions should be taken to _____ the confidentiality of the procedure and of related records. Health care providers who are personally _____ to conception by artificial means are not obligated to participate in procedures.

fertilized

Any _____ egg that has the potential for human life and that will be implanted in the uterus of a woman should not be subjected to laboratory research.

gametes
embryos
sold

social
alternative

The following guidelines should be observed when dealing with frozen embryos: (1) The man and woman who provided the _____ (eggs and sperm) should have control over the frozen _____—whether they should be used by them, donat-ed to others or destroyed (but not _____); (2) Research should be permitted in accordance with the guidelines on fetal research; (3) The providers of the eggs and the sperms should have equal voice in the use of the pre-embryos. Surrogacy does not—for various ethical, _____ and legal reasons—represent a satisfactory reproductive _____ for people who wish to become parents.

availability

could
selection

Physicians should promote informed reproductive choices by counseling prospective parents on the _____ and role of prenatal genetic screening, including reasons for and against screening and the appropriate uses of genetic testing. Physicians _____ participate in genetic selection to prevent, cure, or treat genetic disease, but it would not be ethical to engage in genetic _____ on the basis of non-disease-causing characteristics or traits.

laws

accept

produce

Physicians may ethically perform abortions in accordance with applicable _____ and sound medical practice. A physician personally opposed to abortion is not obli-gated to _____ a patient requesting one. Ethically, health care providers may participate in fetal research if the activities are part of an acceptably designed pro-gram to _____ data which are scientifically valid and significant. The research must conform with the accepted standards of scientific research. No

fees / state
consent

_____ are collected. All federal and _____ laws must be observed. A written, fully informed _____ must be received from the gravid woman or her legal agent.

religious

refuse
job

Physicians may refuse to perform contraceptive sterilization procedures because of _____ or moral objections. Most states have enacted conscience laws permitting physicians, other health care providers, and private hospitals receiving no public funds to _____ to perform sterilization procedures for religious or moral objections without fear of _____ recriminations.

issue
autonomy

HIV
risk

There are innumerable issues and potential issues involving HIV results, ARC, and AIDS, but the primary _____ revolves around confidentiality vs. disclosure. The AMA Judicial Council declared that it is important to respect patient _____ and confidentiality as much as possible. It is important to obtain informed consent, specifically for _____ testing, before testing. A patient may be tested without his/her consent if a health care provider is at _____ for HIV infection because of the occurrence of contact with potentially infected bodily fluids. At-risk patients should be encouraged to obtain testing.

third
cease
notified

Confidentiality may be waived when it is necessary to protect the public health or when necessary to protect individuals, including health care providers, who are endangered by persons infected with HIV. If an infected patient is endangering a _____ party, the physician should attempt to persuade the infected patient to _____ endangering the third party; if that fails, the authorities should be _____; and if they take no action, the physician should notify the endangered third party. (_Note: These actions might be contrary to individual state laws._)

unethical   knowledge
refuses

patient's

Denying treatment to an HIV-infected, HIV-seropositive patient or to a patient who is unwilling to be tested is _____ except in a case in which _____ of the patient's HIV status is vital to the patient's treatment. If a patient _____ after being informed of the physician's medical opinion, the physician would be justified in transferring care to another physician who is willing to abide by the _____ decision about testing.

deformed
quality
severely
parents

With regard to the treatment of severely _____ newborns and other people severely damaged by injury or illness, the _____ of a person's life is one factor to consider in determining treatment. The decision to treat a _____ deformed newborn to the greatest extent possible belongs to the _____. The advice, knowledge and cooperation of the physician should be readily available to the parents.

JUDGMENT

According to your personal and professional judgment, determine whether the situations below are ethical or unethical and indicate your answer by writing an "E" or an "U" in the space provided.

1. ____ A health care provider refuses to participate in in vitro fertilization based on his/her own religious beliefs.
2. ____ A couple with three daughters asks a health care provider to perform prenatal genetic screening in order to ensure that the new baby will be a son; the provider complies.
3. ____ A physician notifies a noncompliant patient that she/he will be withdrawing from the case by a reasonable point in time in the future.
4. ____ A health care provider refuses to continue treatment of a patient who has tested positive for HIV.
5. ____ A physician reports the adverse action of a prescription drug to the Food and Drug Administration.

ANSWERS TO EXERCISES

JUDGMENT

1. E
2. U—*It would not be ethical to engage in genetic selection on the basis of non-disease-causing characteristics or traits.*
3. E
4. U—*Denying treatment to an HIV-infected, HIV-seropositive patient or to a patient who is unwilling to be tested is unethical.*
5. E

Final Examination

1. Obtaining a license as a health care professional by reciprocity is best described as:
   a. being granted a license because the person has been working as a licensed professional although he/she has never met the requirements for licensure.
   b. being granted a license by being licensed in one state and moving to another state which officially recognizes the licensure of the first state as being at least as stringent as its own.
   c. being granted a license by completing an educational program in the field but never meeting the other requirements for licensure.

2. Which statement best reflects the usual different between licensure and certification?
   a. Both licensure and certification are mandatory state credentials.
   b. Licensure is a voluntary state credential, and certification is a mandatory state credential.
   c. Both licensure and certification are voluntary national credentials.
   d. Licensure is a mandatory state credential, and certification is a voluntary credential.

3. Which statement is most correct?
   a. Certification is usually a voluntary credential awarded by a professional group.
   b. A degree or diploma is usually a voluntary credential awarded by a professional group.
   c. A license is usually a voluntary credential awarded by a professional organization.
   d. Certification is usually a mandatory credential awarded by a state.

4. Which statement is most accurate?
   a. All contracts must be in writing in order to be valid and enforceable.
   b. The statute of limitations stipulates which contracts must be in writing in order to be valid and enforceable.
   c. The statute of frauds stipulates which contracts must be in writing in order to be valid and enforceable.
   d. All contracts must be oral in order to be valid and enforceable.

5. Which statement is most correct?
   a. Health care providers are legally forbidden from making guarantees of a favorable outcome to a patient.
   b. Health care providers can be sued for breach of contract if a guarantee of a favorable outcome is made to a patient, and the result does not meet or exceed the quality of the outcome guaranteed by the health care provider.
   c. Health care providers can be sued for negligence if they act with reasonable skill and knowledge in treating a patient, but the result does not meet or exceed the quality of the outcome guaranteed by the health care provider.
   d. In a specific situation, health care providers cannot be sued both for negligence and breach of contract.

6. Which statement is most accurate:
   a. If legal guidelines are followed, either the patient or the health care provider can terminate the patient/health care provider relationship.

b. If legal guidelines are followed, only the patient can terminate the patient/health care provider relationship.

c. If legal guidelines are followed, only the health care provider can terminate the patient/health care provider relationship.

d. Even if legal guidelines are followed, neither the patient nor the health care provider can terminate the patient/health care provider relationship.

7. Abandonment is best defined as:
   a. The unilateral severance by the patient of the patient/health care provider relationship without giving reasonable notice to the health care provider.
   b. The unwillingness of a health care provider to treat nonemergency patients experiencing medical conditions outside the scope of expertise of the provider's specialty.
   c. The unilateral severance by the health care provider of the patient/health care provider relationship without giving reasonable notice to the patient.
   d. The unwillingness of a health care provider to provide free services to those individuals who cannot afford his/her fees.

8. True or false? Notice of a health care provider's desire to withdraw from the care of a patient should not be committed to writing for fear of lawsuit.
   a. True
   b. False

9. Good Samaritan laws:
   a. Shield health care providers from suits alleging ordinary negligence if the provider treats an individual at the scene of an accident.
   b. Forbid health care providers from assisting injured individuals at the scene of an accident.
   c. Require health care providers to provide a certain number of hours of free care every year.
   d. Shield health care providers from suits alleging gross negligence if the provider treats an individual at the scene of an accident.

10. True or false? Patients may limit disclosure to a certain condition, but may not select only certain pieces of information about that condition for release.
    a. True
    b. False

11. The following statements about privileged communication statutes are true except which of the following:
    a. These statutes prohibit a health care provider from testifying about a patient unless the patient consents to the testimony or waives his/her rights under the law.
    b. These statutes are meant to protect the health care provider.
    c. In some jurisdictions, a patient may waive the right to nondisclosure by testifying in court voluntarily or by bringing a lawsuit against the health care provider.

12. The patient's legal right to confidentiality is:
    a. balanced against the health care provider's right to disclose whatever he/she thinks necessary.
    b. absolute and can never be overridden.
    c. not absolute, and can be superseded in limited cases by the public's right to certain information.
    d. balanced against the health care provider's right to protect his/her economic well-being.

13. A patient informs his/her psychiatrist or clinical psychologist that he/she plans to harm a third party. What is the most accurate statement of the legal duty of the psychiatrist or clinical psychologist?
    a. The mental health professional must treat the patient in a non-negligent manner, but owes no duty to any third party and must not divulge the information under any circumstances.
    b. The mental health professional should follow the necessary legal guidelines and withdraw from the case immediately and thus rid himself/herself of any legal duty to anyone.
    c. The mental health professional owes a duty to the third party as well as to the patient, and must act to protect the public welfare as well as the welfare of the patient.

14. True or false? Only the doctor has the legal and ethical duty to respect the patient's right of privacy. Employees of the doctor owe a duty to the doctor, but owe no duty to the patient.
    a. True
    b. False

15. Which of the following is/are not legally able to give an informed consent to a health care provider?
    a. An individual who has been placed under legal disability by court order.
    b. An emancipated minor.
    c. An adult who is in a coma.
    d. All of the above.

16. Which of the following is not necessary for the health care provider to disclose to the patient in order for the patient's consent to be informed?
    a. Alternative treatments and the likely outcome of each such treatment.
    b. Normal risks and hazards inherent in the proposed treatment.
    c. Side effects or complications known normally to occur.
    d. The likelihood that a procedure will be covered by the patient's health insurance.

17. True or false? Health care providers are legally obligated to disclose every risk associated with a method of treatment--regardless of the likelihood of occurrence, permanence, or severity of the risk.
    a. True
    b. False

18. Which of the following is not a situation in which no consent for treatment is required?
    a. The treatment is the only reasonable approach a health care professional could take to a certain disease.
    b. There is a life-threatening emergency.
    c. A court order requiring treatment has been issued.
    d. Because of public policy considerations, the law requires treatment.

19. A tort is:
    a. A civil wrong based on breach of contract.
    b. A criminal wrong.
    c. Both a civil wrong based on breach of contract and a criminal wrong.
    d. A civil wrong other than one based on breach of contract.

20. True of false? A health care provider is held to the standard of care of the most qualified specialist in the area of treatment for which the patient is being treated.
    a. True
    b. False

21. Assault and battery:
    a. constitutes a crime and not a tort.
    b. constitutes a tort and not a crime.
    c. can constitute both a crime and a tort.

22. Which of the following must not be shown in a professional negligence suit against a health care provider?
    a. The health care provider had established a legally valid relationship with the patient and consequently owed the patient the standard of care.
    b. The health care provider exhibited evil intent in dealing with and treating the patient.
    c. The health care provider did not meet the standard of care owed the patient and therefore acted in a negligent manner.
    d. The health care provider's negligence was the proximate cause of the patient's harm.

23. In a professional malpractice suit, the plaintiff must show that the defendant was negligent:
    a. beyond a reasonable doubt.
    b. beyond a shadow of a doubt.
    c. by a preponderance of the evidence.

24. True or false? In a *res ipsa loquitur* situation, it is more difficult for a plaintiff/patient to prove that the defendant/health care provider was negligent.
    a. True
    b. False

25. Which type of damages is awarded as punishment to the wrongdoer for the reckless or malicious nature of the wrongdoing?
    a. Special damages
    b. Nominal damages
    c. Punitive damages
    d. Compensatory damages

26. Which one of the following best describes the principle of *respondeat superior*?
    a. The allied health employee of the employer/health care provider is responsible for the negligence of the employer/health care provider.
    b. Only the employer/health care provider is responsible for the negligence of the allied health employee.
    c. Both the employer/health care provider and the allied health employee can be responsible for the negligence of the allied health employee.
    d. Only the allied health employee is responsible for his/her own negligence.

27. True or false? According to the doctrine of *respondeat superior*, the employer/health care provider is responsible for the actions of the allied health employee which are not within the course and scope of the allied health professional's employment.
    a. True
    b. False

28. A defendant health care provider's attempt to show that he/she was not negligent is an example of:
    a. an affirmative defense
    b. a denial defense
    c. a technical defense

29. True or false? A tolling of the statute of limitations means that the period during which a suit may be filed has run out and it is too late for a plantiff to file a suit.
    a. True
    b. False

30. The legal principle that holds that once an assertion in a lawsuit has been resolved on the basis of facts, it cannot be relitigated by the same parties is called:
    a. *res judicata*
    b. unappealability
    c. *stare decisis*
    d. *laches*

31. True or false? Intentional torts are usually covered by a health care provider's malpractice liability insurance.
    a. True
    b. False

32. Which of the following is *not* an example of insurance fraud?
    a. Billing for services that were not rendered.
    b. Billing for a full fee when deductible and copayments are being waived.
    c. Failing to explain the nature of insurance coverage to a patient.
    d. Using inappropriate codes for insurance billing.

33. True or false? In a situation of suspected child abuse, the parents—not the child—are owed the duty of confidentiality by the health care provider.
    a. True
    b. False

34. Which of the following is usually not an area addressed by public health statutes?
    a. Monitoring water quality.
    b. Ranking health care providers in regard to cost of services they provide.
    c. Ensuring sanitary conditions in public places.
    d. Inspecting establishments in which food and drink are processed and sold.

35. True or false? A body must never be disposed of until a doctor has completed the medical portion of a death certificate, signed it, and transmitted it to the funeral director in charge of the funeral arrangements.
    a. True
    b. False

36. In which of the following cases does the medical examiner usually not have jurisdiction?
    a. The decedent was being treated by a nontraditional health care practitioner and not by an allopathic or osteopathic physician.
    b. The cause of death is unknown.
    c. A violent or criminal act is a suspected cause of death.
    d. The decedent was not attended by a health care provider at the time of death or for a reasonable amount of time preceding death.

37. Chain of custody procedures must be followed when specimens are obtained that might be legally significant. In a chain of custody situation, which of the following is usually not a duty of laboratory and office personnel?
    a. Observe the collection of the specimen from the patient.
    b. Completely and accurately label the specimen and complete, sign, and date the form.
    c. Obtain the patient's initials on the form to indicate his/her verification of the specimen's authenticity.
    d. Inform the attorney of the decedent that the chain of custody procedures are being followed.
    e. Place the top copy of the form in the clear plastic bag with the specimen, make sure the patient's name is visible, and seal the bag.

38. Taking into account the fact that state laws vary, which of the following legal provisions regarding involuntary commitment of individuals with documented or suspected mental illness does not appear in most statutes?
    a. A patient should be urged to commit himself/herself voluntarily before involuntary commitment procedures are initiated.
    b. A patient should be promised that his/her confinement will be of a short duration, and that no unpleasant things will happen.
    c. A doctor must certify to the need of commitment, and the certification must be based on a valid and recent medical examination.
    d. A patient must be notified in advance that he/she is to be committed, and why this must be done.
    e. A formal hearing must be conducted, with the patient having the right to assistance of legal counsel at relevant times.

39. True or false? To administer a drug is to give it to the patient in a container for later use.
    a. True
    b. False

40. Which of the following is not a precaution medical office personnel can take to prevent controlled substances from falling into the hands of addicts or unauthorized handlers?
    a. Prescription blanks should not be left in unattended places within the office.
    b. When the doctor's bag is in the office, it should be stored in a place inaccessible to any patients.
    c. Prescription blanks can be numbered and issued consecutively to facilitate the detection of theft.
    d. People from out of town should be prescribed controlled substances with fewer questions asked than in a normal situation because of stressful situations encountered by travelers.

41. Which of the following is generally not a primary purpose of patient records?
    a. To serve as an aid to practicing medicine.
    b. To serve as a document that doctors can use to give informed consent to treatment modalities.
    c. To function as a tool in medical research and teaching.
    d. To serve as an aid to communication.
    e. The function as a legal document.

42. Which of the following statements is not correct?
    a. Records initiated and developed in a hospital belong to the hospital.
    b. Records developed by a doctor during the course of private office practice belong to the doctor; the patient has a legal interest in his/her records, and has a right to see and/or obtain a copy of his/her record.
    c. Records initiated and developed in a clinic belong to the clinic owners.
    d. Records developed by a doctor during the course of private office practice belong to the patient; the doctor has a legal interest in the patient's records, and has a right to maintain copies and make any necessary updates to the record.

43. True or false? Although medical records should be kept at least until germane statutes of limitations have expired, because statutes of limitations are extended for so many different reasons, it is preferable to keep records indefinitely.
    a. True
    b. False

44. Which is the preferred policy?
    a. Normal or negative findings are not included in patient records.
    b. Normal or negative findings are included in patient records only if the patient has a question about the outcome of a test.
    c. Normal or negative findings are routinely included in patient records.
    d. Normal or negative findings are included only in patient records which are subject to peer review.

45. Which of the following should not be included in a standard patient record?
    a. Information about the patient's payment history.
    b. Notation of telephone inquiries of a medical nature, along with advice given.
    c. The patient's name, address, telephone number, date of birth, and marital status.
    d. Notation of missed appointments and action taken.
    e. Special instructions (for example, instructions regarding home care, special diet, weight control, personal habits, physical exercise).

46. True or false? It is permissible for a health care provider to refuse to release a patient's medical record because of the patient's failure to pay a bill from the provider.
    a. True
    b. False

47. True or false? Since the purpose of the Occupational Safety and Health Act is to ensure that employees are provided with a workplace that is free from recognized hazards that cause serious injury or death, the OSHA law imposes legal obligations on employers only, and not on employees.
    a. True
    b. False

48. True of false? Employers must offer hepatitis B vaccine free of charge only to every full-time employee who can be reasonably anticipated to have contact with blood or other potentially infectious material.
    a. True
    b. False

49. An employee is correctly classified as nonexempt according to the Fair Labor Standards Act. There are no relevant state laws. Which of the following would be legally permissible or mandatory if the nonexempt employee worked 50 hours during a week?
    a. The employer could pay the employee for 40 hours and give the employee ten hours off the next week as compensatory time.
    b. The employer would have to pay the employee time and a half for the 10 hours exceeding 40 hours per week.
    c. As long as there is a clear statement in the employee policy and procedures manual that is distributed to all employees and that all employees are required to read, the employer may either pay time and a half for hours exceeding 40 per week, may give compensatory time in lieu of overtime or may establish some other equitable policy.
    d. As long as there is a signed agreement between employer and employee, the remuneration for the 10 hours exceeding 40 per week can be handled in an equitable and mutually agreeable manner.

50. True or false? All salaried employees are automatically considered exempt according to federal law, and all employees paid by the hour are considered nonexempt personnel.
    a. True
    b. False

51. True or false? In labor law issues, it is permissible for a state to establish jurisdictional standards that differ from federal law, and to establish standards that are stricter than the federal law.
    a. True
    b. False

52. Which of the following criteria can be utilized for hiring, promotion, termination, and other employment decisions?
    a. age
    b. race
    c. sex
    d. competence
    e. religion

53. Attributes such as height and ability to lift heavy objectives can be established as requirements for all employment positions without fear of legal entanglements.
    a. True
    b. False

54. Which of the following is a legal question to ask during an employment interview?
    a. What is the highest level of education you have attained?
    b. Do you have any children?
    c. Have you ever been arrested?
    d. What is your maiden name?

55. True or false? The Age Discrimination in Employment Act of 1967, a federal statute, only protects individuals within a certain age range from age discrimination.
    a. True
    b. False

56. True or false? *Quid pro quo* sexual harassment is defined as the creation of an environment that is intimidating, hostile, or offensive, and which interferes with the individual's ability to perform creatively or effectively on the job.
    a. True
    b. False

57. Which of the following statements about the Americans with Disabilities Act (ADA) is true?
    a. The law covers employees with all disabilities, whether minor and nonchronic or substantial and impacting major life activities.
    b. An employer is legally required to give preference in hiring and promotion decisions to disabled individuals.
    c. An employer can dismiss a disabled employee whose behavior is disruptive, or whose performance is unacceptable.
    d. All possible accommodations must be made for the disabled employee. Cost is not a factor because the expense can be deducted for income tax purposes.

58. Which of the following is not a reason for which unpaid, job-protected leave must be given for eligible employees?
    a. For a serious health condition that makes the employee unable to perform his/her job.
    b. For the employee to explore an alternative career which would result in the employee earning a higher salary and more completely fulfilling his/her potential.
    c. To enable an employee to care for his/her child after birth, adoption, or foster care placement.
    d. To enable an employee to care for a spouse, child, or parent who has a serious health condition.

59. True or false? An employee taking a permissible unpaid leave authorized by the Family and Medical Leave Act of 1993 cannot lose any benefit that accrued prior to the start of the employee's leave.
    a. True
    b. False

60. True or false? Generally, it is not illegal under the various fair credit statutes to discriminate against individuals who receive public assistance.
    a. True
    b. False

61. Which of the following is not considered an ethical fee according to the AMA's Principles of Medical Ethics, even if the patient is notified in advance?
    a. A fee for completing multiple or complex insurance forms.
    b. A fee for missed appointments that have not been cancelled within a specific time.
    c. Interest or finance charges.
    d. A charge for the costs of photocopying records requested by the patient.
    e. A fee for referring a patient to a specialist.

62. True or false? A truth in lending statement is required by Regulation Z only if interest is charged?
    a. True
    b. False

63. Which of the following is not an objective of the federal bankruptcy laws?
    a. To provide a fair method of distributing a debtor's assets among all creditors.
    b. To encourage people who are incapable of paying their debts to keep working rather than giving up their jobs and receiving public assistance.
    c. To provide insolvent debtors with relief and protection from creditors who harass and threaten the debtors.
    d. To encourage employers to not give pay increases to employees who are hopelessly mired in frivolous debt.

64. Which of the following is not a pleading in a lawsuit?
    a. Writ of mandamus
    b. Reply
    c. Complaint
    d. Answer

65. True or false? An interrogatory is a statement made under oath by a witness or potential witness in a question and answer form.
    a. True
    b. False

66. True or false? An appeal to a higher court must be based on an issue of law, rather than on an issue of fact.
    a. True
    b. False

67. True or false? A joint screening panel is intended to be a complete substitute for the litigation process, whereas arbitration is a way of evaluating the merits of a claim and making a recommendation as to what the next step should be in resolving a dispute.
    a. True
    b. False

68. Which of the following is not a fundamental principle of medical ethics?
    a. The individual patient's welfare is of prime concern.
    b. In making a difficult decision, the health care provider must balance the welfare of his/her patient with his/her own welfare.
    c. Medical privileges must not be abused.
    d. Except for certain exceptions, information acquired by health care providers during the course of treatment must be kept confidential.
    e. The health care provider has an obligation to inform and instruct patients.

69. True or false? Health care providers may advertise, but may not disseminate inaccurate, untrue, or mis-leading information.
    a. True
    b. False

70. Which of the following is a true statement about the relationship between medical law and medical ethics?
    a. Because they are not sanctioned by the state, principles of ethics delineate the lowest standards of conduct that nevertheless fall within the boundaries of the law.
    b. Violations of ethical principles in and of themselves can result in sanctions by state or federal gov-ernmental authorities.
    c. Both medical laws and medical ethics attempt to integrate the needs, goals, and behaviors of individ-uals and society.

71. True or false? With the procedure known as Artificial Insemination Homologous (AIH), in which the woman's husband provides the sperm, there is no legal question about the legitimacy of the biological offspring.
    a. True
    b. False

72. True or false? All institutions, hospitals, hospices, HMOs, nursing facilities, and home care programs receiving funds from Medicare and Medicaid are required to give all adult patients written information about their right to accept or refuse medical and surgical treatment.
    a. True
    b. False

73. According to an AMA Judicial Council Opinion, a physician should never expose incompetent, corrupt, dishonest, or unethical conduct by another member of the profession.
    a. True
    b. False

74. Legitimate charges of abandonment could NOT be made in which of the following instances?
    a. cessation of treatment by a substitute physician "covering for" the patient's actual physician
    b. a delivery performed by a substitute physician "covering for" the patient's actual physician
    c. a postsurgical inpatient was not visited by the physician for three days following surgery
    d. a and c
    e. b and c

75. A claim of negligence is valid when
    a. a patient suffers a permanent disability following surgery
    b. the Canterbury Rule is applied
    c. a physician withholds information about material risks of treatment
    d. a patient refuses treatment and the physician complies with that wish

76. Statutes that prevent disclosure of patient information by physicians serve to protect the
    a. attorney who represents the patient
    b. courts against perjury
    c. physician and his/her interests
    d. patient and his/her interests
    e. hospital and its interests

77. The "consideration" element in a physician–patient contract must meet which of the following criteria?
    a. must be in writing and signed by both parties
    b. may be in force by implication
    c. specifies the exact services to be performed
    d. specifies the exact charge to be levied for treatment
    e. specifies the duration of the contract period

78. The reasonable physician standard is
    a. the standard of patient care used to determine negligence
    b. a rule of thumb for establishing treatment charges
    c. the defense against assault and battery
    d. a statute

79. Commonly, state medical practice acts contain stipulations relating to all of the following EXCEPT
    a. who can practice medicine
    b. what the practice of medicine is
    c. reciprocity across state lines
    d. the structure of the state board of medical examiners
    e. the retirement of physicians

80. Litigation involving physicians and their patients most often falls under which of the following categories of law?
    a. criminal
    b. tort
    c. consumer protection
    d. family
    e. public

81. Which of the following is NOT cause for a physician to lose the license to practice medicine?
    a. conviction of a felony
    b. inappropriate criticism of other physicians
    c. drug abuse

82. Procedural law refers to the "rules of the game" while substantive law is concerned with
    a. rights and responsibilities in legal relationships
    b. who was actually negligent in a malpractice suit
    c. how much money is awarded in a civil dispute
    d. whether a judge is unbiased in handling a case
    e. the implementation of court proceedings

83. When physicians practice defensive medicine, they may
    a. not order laboratory tests for fear of what may be discovered
    b. order more laboratory tests than are necessary to cover every contingency
    c. not treat a patient with a condition that they cannot "cure"
    d. all of the above
    e. b and c

84. Informed consent means that
    a. the patient understands the proposed treatment
    b. the physician has described the proposed treatment
    c. the risks of the procedure are written down for the patient
    d. the physician is qualified to perform the treatment
    e. the treatment is experimental

85. An adult patient may choose his/her own physician and/or refuse medical treatment because
    a. he/she believes the physician cannot help him/her
    b. he/she believes the treatment is dangerous
    c. it is his/her legal right
    d. "Man is the master of his own body"
    e. All of the above are correct.

86. The term *subpoena* means
    a. the person served is being sued
    b. come to testify
    c. a malpractice suit has been filed
    d. the physician must testify alone
    e. release the patient's medical record

87. Common law decisions are made by
    a. legislatures
    b. Congress
    c. city councils
    d. judges
    e. city ordinances

88. Which of the following types of patient information CANNOT be released without the patient's consent?
    a. death
    b. birth
    c. nontherapeutic abortion
    d. a gunshot wound

89. A surgical consent form usually contains
    a. a release for procedures which the surgeon may consider necessary
    b. a guarantee of results to be obtained
    c. blank spaces
    d. the name of the anesthesiologist

90. Trust between physician and patient make the relationship which of the following types?
    a. *caveat emptor*
    b. voluntary
    c. fiduciary
    d. platonic
    e. perpetual

91. A material risk is one that
    a. a reasonable person would consider significant
    b. might result in the patient's loss of property
    c. could result in permanent disability

92. A letter withdrawing from a case should contain
    a. the physician's signature
    b. the patient's medical record
    c. the bill for services rendered
    d. the recommendation that the patient correct his/her misbehavior and return to see the physician

93. The patient's right to privacy is NOT violated when which of the following actions are not authorized by the patient?
    a. medical information is given by the physician to the parents of a 14-year-old patient
    b. an Eagle Scout troop observes surgery from outside a glass partition
    c. medical information is given by the physician to the parents of an emancipated minor
    d. all of the above

94. A specialty board or professional organization grants which type of recognition for satisfactorily meeting its standards for entering into practice?
    a. continuing education units
    b. a diploma
    c. certification
    d. a degree
    e. licensure

95. Professional malpractice and personal injury fall into which of the following areas of law?
   a. private
   b. public
   c. criminal
   d. family
   e. property

96. A physician may limit care in relation to
   a. type of service provided
   b. how services will be provided
   c. locale of practice
   d. when services are provided
   e. all of the above

97. An emancipated minor is which of the following?
   a. a person aged 18-21 years
   b. a minor who has been told by his/her parents to leave home
   c. a minor in a correctional institution/school
   d. a minor child who supports himself/herself and lives independently
   e. a person aged 16-18 years who lives away from home

98. The rules of informed consent require that the patient understand each of the following EXCEPT
   a. potential side effects
   b. the probable results of having no treatment
   c. the specific reason for each step of the procedure
   d. the likelihood of risks occurring
   e. the permanence of potential complications

99. An appeal of a judge's decision must be based upon
   a. a witness' change of testimony
   b. the jury's decision
   c. an issue of law
   d. additional damages to the plaintiff
   e. a witness that was overlooked

100. Which of the following is NOT an obligation of a patient in the physician-patient relationship?
   a. to tell the truth
   b. to pay his/her medical bills
   c. to take his/her medicine
   d. to carry health insurance
   e. to keep appointments